DATE DUE

GOD BLESS PAWNBROKERS

God Bless Pawnbrokers

✳

PETER SCHWED

✳

✳ ✳ ✳

DODD, MEAD & COMPANY
NEW YORK

The poem by Marguerite Wilkinson is reprinted by permission of the Dial Press.

Library of Congress Cataloging in Publication Data

Schwed, Peter.
   God bless pawnbrokers.

   1. Provident Loan Society of New York.
I. Title.
HG2084.N7S33   332.3'4   75-22252
ISBN 0-396-07222-4

For my Antonia

Acknowledgments

Several people have kindly given me their time and help in pursuing some of the factual information about The Provident Loan Society of New York that appears in this book. I am particularly grateful to my old boss, E. Munroe Bates, who dictated three tapes from his sickbed in Florida. I also was fortunate enough to be able to interview two old friends who were contemporaries of mine when I worked for the Society, James Werhle and Frank Leonard. Both began their careers there before I was hired, and stayed on for decades after I left, so their long-term views were a great help to me.

The present administration of the Provident has been gracious and cooperative in letting me see data and other information that it would have been difficult for me to lay my hands upon otherwise. No restriction was placed upon any use of this material, and I have availed myself freely of this generous privilege. Similarly, much of the historical background of the Society in Chapter 1 is taken from a pamphlet written in 1932 by Rolf Nugent, then of the Russell Sage Foundation, and some of it is verbatim. Finally,

I'd like to thank David F. Cohen for sharing with me his fund of information about commercial pawnbrokers.

But for the most part, the stories, anecdotes, and descriptions of the times are my own, hopefully accurate, memories of forty years ago. I told some of them casually one day at lunch to Scott Meredith, my literary agent, and before coffee he had made me promise to write this book. So if you enjoy it, he receives an acknowledgment too. And if you don't, it's Scott's fault.

P.S.

God bless pawnbrokers!
They are quiet men.
You may go once—
You may go again—
They do not question
As a brother might;
They never say
What they think is right;
They never hint
All you ought to know;
Lay your treasure down,
Take your cash and go,
Fold your ticket up
In a secret place
With your shaken pride
And your shy disgrace,
Take the burly world
By the throat again—
God bless pawnbrokers!
They are quiet men.

—*Marguerite Wilkinson*

Contents

Prologue: *The Unthinkable Ripoff*   13

1: *You've Got to Have Heart!*   21

2: *The Aspirin Age and Me*   42

3: *The Borrowers' Tales*   56

4: *The Quiet Men*   77

5: *How to Become a Diamond Expert*   92

6: *All Is Not Diamonds That Glitters*   119

7: *Sold at Auction*   147

8: *Curiouser and Curiouser*   166

9: *The Distant Drum*   177

10: *Pop Goes the Weasel!*   193

PROLOGUE

The Unthinkable Ripoff

On February 17, 1969, Sheldon Saltzman of Jamaica, Queens, and Thomas Palermo of Astoria, Queens, were due to appear at 10 o'clock in the morning in State Supreme Court in St. George, Staten Island, to stand trial for the $11,000 robbery of two widowed sisters on the island.

They actually arrived in court almost two hours late, at 11:45, apologized politely, and explained that they had been involved in an auto accident.

It happened on that same day that one of the biggest and most spectacular jewelry thefts in recent history took place between 10:15 and 10:45. Two men entered the Jamaica branch of The Provident Loan Society of New York and held up the manager and the other two office employees at gunpoint. Over 3,000 pieces of diamond and other precious jewelry, whose retail value was estimated between $4 million and $6 million, plus approximately $8,000 in cash, was stuffed into two large airline bags by the robbers, who then disappeared down Hillside Avenue into the wilds of Long Island.

Because they had not appeared in court on time, Justice

Michael Kern remanded Saltzman and Palermo to jail for the remainder of the Staten Island robbery trial, and canceled their bail. Subsequently he meted out a twenty-five-year prison sentence for Palermo and fifteen years for Saltzman.

Meanwhile, the police, noting the coincidence of the date, time, and location, had been investigating the pair's possible connection with The Provident Loan Society stickup. There was certainly no record of any auto accident in Jamaica such as Palermo and Saltzman had described.

Three months later, on May 22, the police cracked the Loan Society case when the young woman cashier in the Provident's office, Joanne Tanner, was able to identify the two men. She had always claimed she would be able to do so if she ever had the opportunity, and when presented with a batch of "mug shots," she unerringly picked out photos of Palermo and Saltzman. They then entered pleas of guilt and subsequently engaged in extensive negotiations with the District Attorney's office to have leniency extended to them if they cooperated in the recovery of The Provident Loan Society's stolen goods. Finally, late in October, Palermo led the police to a car parked at 37th Street and First Avenue in New York. In its trunk they found a suitcase weighing 120 pounds, loaded with diamond rings, bracelets, pins, emeralds, rubies, sapphires, pearls, and watches. Approximately 90 percent of the total theft, both in number of articles and in value, was in that suitcase. Of course the Provident Loan people were tremendously relieved and grateful to the police, but they did have a little problem left on their hands.

When an article is pledged, a tag is securely attached to it that specifically relates it to the number on the loan ticket issued to the borrower; which in turn bears the borrower's name and the means of relating it to his or her address. The thieves had removed and destroyed all of these tags, so the Provident had recovered more than 3,000 pieces of jewelry that had no direct identification connecting them to the owners! The basic description of a piece of jewelry as written on the loan ticket is very general. For example, a single-stone diamond solitaire ring is merely noted as "Diamond Ring," and a bracelet, let us say, as "Diamond Bracelet, 43 diamonds." There is no specific description of a stone's size or color or characteristics on the ticket, and one has to proceed another step into the records of the transaction to correlate this information to the loan in question. The ramifications of trying to sort things out under these circumstances would have made Sherlock Holmes throw up his hands and go into the textile business. It was almost unquestionably the biggest and most complicated jigsaw puzzle in history, but The Provident Loan Society staff finally pieced it together.

The later developments of this story, which were hotly contested in court while Palermo and Saltzman were beginning their jail sentences for the Staten Island heist, and which still are not finally settled, do not relate to what this book is all about. So let's leave Messrs. Palermo and Saltzman forever at this point, although it is intriguing to wonder if they actually planned to crowd in The Provident Loan Society caper that shining hour. Was it just an immediate and inspired decision made over shared breakfast coffee, since there was some time to kill before having to catch the Staten Island ferry? I doubt if we'll ever know, and it doesn't really matter.

For the real point of the affair is that it happened to The Provident Loan Society of New York, which for the better part of a century had represented the utmost imaginable in propriety and security. No breath of scandal had ever even faintly touched its reputation. And far from proclaiming its good works, the Society had an adamant policy against even favorable publicity. Suddenly here it had experienced one of the biggest jewel robberies in history, and newspaper accounts were in all the papers, including the *Daily News* with pictures! It was absolutely unthinkable!

It's possible that the more mischievous of the gods looked down and smiled, as it is said to occur. But the benign spirits of such departed souls as Robert W. deForest, James Speyer, Otto T. Bannard, Jacob H. Schiff, Frederick H. Ecker, Seth Low, Cornelius Vanderbilt, Henry R. Beekman, Percy Rockefeller, George F. Baker, Charles F. Cox, William E. Dodge, Isaac Newton Seligman, Bishop Greer, Felix Warburg, and J. P. Morgan must have wept. For they had been among the thirty or so tremendously distinguished financiers who, as a contribution to public service, had some seventy-five years before founded The Provident Loan Society. They had set forth the impeccable standards under which it would operate, and then with justifiable pride served without compensation on its directorate. They had seen it render the most unique of business dealings for the needy, mixed in with some of the most romantic and remarkable. No one made any money out of the Provident's huge lending business, apart from the modest salaries earned by the working employees: It was a nonprofit organization whose surplus earnings each year were distributed to charities. Every business transaction, from the loan of one dollar to the loan running into six figures, was handled in the same quiet, unpublicized, impeccable fashion. Readers with fresh memories of Watergate, readers raised throughout years of so many examples of shoddy wheeling and dealing, readers who themselves have come to regard padded expense accounts and dubious income tax deductions as the ordinary way of life, may well scarcely believe how scrupulously the affairs of The Provident Loan Society were conducted. It was truly like Caesar's wife—above suspicion. That anything should occur so shocking and inimical to its borrowers' interests as a major robbery was practically sacrilege, and it had a lasting effect upon something that had seemed as solid and eternal as the pyramids.

GOD BLESS PAWNBROKERS

"Let us all be happy and live within our means, even if we have to borrow the money to do it with."

—Artemus Ward

CHAPTER 1

You've Got to Have Heart!

There is an old joke about a man who was trying to raise a certain amount of money, which he needed desperately, by pawning his watch. He wasn't succeeding very well with the one-eyed pawnbroker until he poured out his sad story of need. The only way he finally knew he was going to get the required amount was when he saw the gleam of sympathy in the pawnbroker's glass eye.

Pawnbroking, the oldest method of lending money in history, has existed in every type of civilization. It appears, for example, in the Old Testament, and if a person has to borrow, there is much to be said in its favor. For one thing, it is the quickest method of lending money, for a loan is made solely upon the estimated value of the collateral offered as security. No credit investigation need be made by the lender, eliminating the sort of embarrassment that usually arises when friends, relatives, or employers have to be approached. Additionally, since the lender theoretically has his protection in the value of the pledged article (even though it may not work out that way if the article is not redeemed), there is no obligation on the part of the borrower ever to repay if he chooses not to do so. And if he doesn't, he stands to collect any surplus money that the article realizes when it is sold.

Yet throughout the ages, pawnbrokers and pawnshops have been associated with sordidness and ridicule in the minds of most people. Shakespeare contributed his share toward that attitude with his creation of Shylock demanding his pound of flesh. So did the Medici family with its three-ball sign. More realistically for their reputation in modern times, the general run of pawnshops existed in ramshackle, dirty, small shops tucked away in ghetto districts and honky-tonk streets, lending money at usurious interest rates to pathetic, ignorant, down-and-out borrowers. There were some respectable "uncles" who ran a decent business and dealt honestly, but they were few and far between, and even they charged right up to the maximum interest rates the law allowed: 36 percent a year. It certainly was not the sort of business that you'd want to see your daughter marry into.

In 1894, after two previous catastrophic years, a financial panic and business depression reached a crisis only surpassed by the 1929 crash and the subsequent years of the 1930's. Unemployment skyrocketed, people did not have enough money to buy food, and charitable organizations were swamped with appeals for help. Public and private relief agencies were altogether inadequate to alleviate conditions. Their dispensations did not exceed $10 million a year in a population of over two and a half million people. No one had a friend then at Chase Manhattan, and there were no such things as credit cards. To get even the smallest loan—or, for that matter, a big one—a person had to have some form of collateral such as stocks, bonds, or real estate to put up as security. On the whole, that meant seeking out the pawnbroker as a last resort for most people. And the pawnbroker's ancient reputation for sharp practices, usury, and exploitation was well developed at that time.

So New York's outstanding private charities' administration, the Charity Organization Society, headed at the time by Robert W. deForest, started to investigate the possibility of setting up a semiphilanthropic agency to make loans to people in need. Mr. Alfred Bishop Mason, a C.O.S. member and later one of the founders of the Provident Loan, stated the concept this way: ". . . There is still one gap in our line of defenses against misery which needs to be filled. We should unite to act as pawnbrokers; lend money at low rates on good security to approved borrowers among the poor; and so divorce the three balls from the three Furies. . . . I would have a pawnshop which should be the poor man's bank, the place to which he could go when he has been robbed of his tools, when he has been smitten with sickness, or when he saw before him a chance of rising from man to master by borrowing a little capital to start a little shop. . . . Borrowing is often the greatest of necessities for the poor. They pay for it the price of the greatest luxuries. Let [us] . . . build up in New York a great institution where it shall not be shame and ruin to borrow and where loss of self-respect shall not make a part of every pledge."

James Speyer, one of the group of public-spirited wealthy men who headed the C.O.S., undertook to go to Europe and study the operation of the Monts de Piété, the municipal pawnshops. Upon his return he wrote: "Public institutions governed by business principles to assist poor people in temporary need to make small loans at reasonable rates on articles of daily use have been in existence in Europe for nearly three hundred years. The earliest example of such an institution is furnished by the city of Freising, Germany, in 1198 and the city of Salans, in Burgundy, in 1350 where some philanthropic citizens combined to raise a fund for the above purpose. These institutions exist today in Italy, Spain, France, Austria, Germany and Holland under government or municipal supervision. . . . Why should not such a society, profiting by the experience gained elsewhere, succeed in New York City?"

The largest Mont de Piété at that time was the Crédit Municipal de Paris, known to Frenchmen affectionately as "my aunt" (as opposed to the American appellation of "uncle," which may say something about American attitudes before Women's Lib). It was the major factor that enabled starving artists, poets, and lovers to pay something down on the rent, buy a bottle of vin ordinarie and an Alsatian sausage, and carry on until next time. Spurred by the seriousness of the business depression and by Mr. Speyer's enthusiasm for the project, the Charity Organization Society went to work.

A meeting was called and $40,000 was subscribed to a loan fund to get things started. Three weeks later a bill was introduced in the state legislature chartering The Provident Loan Society. It passed the Senate by a unanimous vote, but was resisted in the House by the organized opposition of loan sharks.

But the great metropolitan newspapers rallied unanimously to support the project with editorials that read like this:

"Rich and charitable men are willing to advance money in order to confer a great and lasting benefit upon people

who may be from time to time in urgent need of money."
The New York Times

"The Society is essentially benevolent in the true sense . . .
its motive is entirely unselfish." *New York Tribune*

"This measure is purely charitable." *New York World*

Public opinion forced the passage of the act, and it was
signed by the governor soon afterwards. By May 1894 an
office supplied rent-free by the Charity Organization Society
had been remodeled and equipped, employees hired, and the
doors were thrown open for business.

It was instantly apparent that New York needed this new
opportunity and was eager to take advantage of it. Within
three weeks almost $20,000 had been lent out. Since the aver-
age loan was only about $10, almost 2,000 people had flocked
into the small office to raise a little cash. Both larger quarters
and more capital were needed right away, and the original
subscribers were asked to increase their contributions and to
solicit others. Another $60,000 was raised, giving the Society
a working capital of $100,000.

The original donors were given a most unusual document,
called a Certificate of Contribution. Legally it meant just
that and no more: They had *given* their money to the Provident Loan and there was no obligation either to pay interest
on it or to ever liquidate the principal. Yet very substantial
sums were raised in this manner, sufficient to finance the
Society's operations originally and for decades to come; each
holder received the maximum 6 percent interest that was set
out in the document as a *possibility* if the trustees decided
to pay interest to the contributors out of earnings. As long as
Certificates of Contribution were in existence, they always

continued to pay 6 percent, which was an admirable return for invested money in those days. The certificates were admitted to trading on the New York Stock Exchange and were affectionately dubbed "Provident Perpetual Sixes." A lot of conservative investors were disappointed when they finally were called in at face value in the 1930's, when the Society's business was so big that earnings more than supplied working capital. The certificates had been as safe as money in the bank—safer in view of the bank closings in 1933—and banks weren't paying anything like 6 percent interest then.

Beginning with the opening of a first branch office on the Lower East Side, the Provident kept expanding its services through the years. As it prospered, new sites were purchased and other branch buildings were constructed.

The sites chosen during the organization's growth through the first decade of the century centered upon the poorer areas of the city, particularly in Manhattan's Lower East Side and comparable ghetto districts in Brooklyn. By 1910 the Society was ready to expand still further, not only with more such offices, including a couple in the Bronx, but also with new branches in the better residential and business locations of the city. By 1920 it had thirteen local offices spread over the three boroughs, all open for business and thriving.

"Thriving" is a modest word for it. In the Society's first full year of operation, back in 1894–1895, it had extended approximately 20,000 loans amounting roughly to $350,000. Five years later it was accommodating 100,000 people to the tune of $2 million in loans annually. In 1910 the figures were almost 400,000 and $12 million. The number of pledgers had not changed substantially by 1920, but the amount loaned out annually was up to $30 million.

The decade that followed witnessed even more growth and expansion. Half a dozen new branches were created, and by the very early 1930's, more than half a million people were pledging articles to the amount of $40 million annually. That was the peak figure in the Provident's long history, for the dollar loan balance has never been so large since then. However, the effect of the 1929 stock market crash and the ensuing great Depression of the 1930's set up two contrasting effects upon the operations of the Society. Its services were required even more desperately by the suddenly stricken community, and the number of new loans made each year surged steadily upward through the decade, reaching a high of three-quarters of a million pledgers in 1939.

The explanation of the apparent paradox of why the loan balance declined a few million dollars annually during this period, despite the remarkable increase in number of customers, is obvious. The Depression made the bottom fall out on prices of everything, and certainly jewelry was no exception. Knowing that people were less likely to redeem their goods in such an economic climate, and that the greater number of forfeited loans going to auction sale would unquestionably fetch much poorer prices than in the past, the Society instituted an extremely cautious lending policy. Whereas the average loan in 1929 had been almost $90 per transaction, it was down to $47 in 1939.

Despite the effect that this had upon dollar volume, The Provident Loan Society performed its primary mission during the dark years of the Thirties to the greatest extent it ever did. Its true goal, the rendering of service to the truly needy in as great numbers as possible, assuredly was carried out beyond the wildest dreams of the founders. Even more offices were established, finally reaching a high of twenty-two branches operating at one time during the 1930's.

The founders believed that a Provident Loan office should not only be run like a conservative and dignified bank but that its exterior and interior appearance should reflect that intent. The architecture of new buildings was planned with a more or less uniform appearance, not unlike small Grecian temples. Each office had a porter, whose job was to keep the place spotless and make the marble glow and the brass doorknobs gleam. Inside, each office looked the way banks used to look when Bonnie and Clyde were doing business with them, which is the way nervous depositers like myself still would prefer them to be. Solid stone and marble, few windows and those very small, thick walls that would have to be blasted through before a robber would ever reach the actual vault itself. Banks and The Provident Loan's offices were not styled by interior decorators with a penchant toward glass counters and partitions: they were reassuringly *sturdy*.

The office staff that served the public in those days consisted entirely of men, and while each man was permitted to retain the trousers he wore that day, he hung up his jacket and donned a black one that the Society had made to his measurement. He wore a white shirt and any color tie he desired, as long as its color ranged from gray through dark blue to black. A solid-colored tie was considered best, but the dressier members of the staff wouldn't draw raised eyebrows if they affected a tie with a pattern as long as the pattern was small and neat. No long hair, of course. The model for proper appearance might well have been the mortician, except Provident employees did not sport carnations in their buttonholes.

Obviously there was no trace of the pawnbroker's traditional three balls hanging over the entrances. The only way an uninformed passerby could figure out what in the world went on inside those elegant, modest, mausoleum-looking buildings was by reading the small, discreet, beautifully lettered signs: "The Provident Loan Society of New York— Loans on Jewelry, Silverware and Other Personal Property." The name of the Society was almost unknown, particularly in the poorer non-English-speaking districts, but everyone knew where the "Penny Pein (pawn) Bank" was located. Only among borrowers in those offices was the word "pawn" used. The Provident's nomenclature for a transaction is that an article is "pledged," and its staff winces ever so slightly if a customer innocently inquires, "What can I hock this for?"

All of this may strike today's reader as ridiculously stuffy and not the sort of thing that made empire builders flourish. The fact of the matter is that empire builders were likely to be on the stuffy side, and with good reason: It worked for them. The Provident Loan had no ambition to build an empire, and clearly acted in everything with the public's needs in mind, but it became enormously successful in the process. The Society so dominated the field that, at the height of the Great Depression of the 1930's, it did considerably more business in New York City than all licensed pawnbrokers put together. It was lending approximately $40 million annually to well over half a million people, more than ten times the annual business done by the Crédit Municipal de Paris, which had been its model.

Sites for new offices, particularly in the business and better residential sections of the city, were carefully chosen to preserve a customer's privacy and lessen the chance of embarrassment for him or her. They were located very near active centers, but invariably a block or so away from the actual heart of the area. That lessened the chance that Mr. Big or Mrs. Dowager would be spotted going through the doors by a hostile or catty acquaintance. (I don't know if the geniuses who run the Off Track Betting offices ever considered this point in selecting their sites, but they well might.) There is no reason why a loan, based upon the pledge of jewelry, should be considered any more shameful than a mortgage on a house, but many people view it so. As a result, in addition to establishing the offices a short distance away from the crowds, the Society extends private individual accommodations to a borrower who, for security or confidential reasons, specially requests it. This is only likely to happen when very spectacular and valuable articles are being offered.

But the prime intent of the Provident is to render its services to the needy, and making thousands of very small and unprofitable loans is its important mission. At the height of its activity during the hard times of the Thirties, when so many people were desperate for funds for food, shelter, clothing, and emergency situations such as sickness and death, almost two-thirds of its loans were for less than $50. The interest on that sum for the average life of the loan did not clear the cost of the physical operations involved in appraising, writing a loan ticket and paying out the money, wrapping and storing the collateral, and then doing the whole thing again in reverse when the article was redeemed. Almost one-fifth of these loans actually were for less than $10; on that sum the interest amounted to no more than a few coins and showed a proportionately greater loss for the Provident on the transaction. There is not a lending organization I know of, other than the Society, that sets no realistically profitable figure as its minimum loan, for the rest are in the business of making a profit. The Provident will make a $1 loan, and would long since have been insolvent if larger loans had not yielded enough to more than cover the vast number of small unprofitable pledges. Yet these small loans are exactly what the Provident was created for. The Society has accumulated large sums over the years as surplus, despite making so many loans that are losers. Yet only working capital for the subsequent year is retained, and all profits are annually distributed among several major charities in the city. If and when the Society ever closes its doors and liquidates, its remaining assets also would be distributed to those charities.

To these charity organizations, to those who gave the Society their time and thought free of charge, and to those who contributed funds when the success of the undertaking was extremely dubious, the Provident is a philanthropy. But in its relationship to borrowers it has always been conducted as a business institution, albeit a nonprofit and often marvelously cooperative and understanding one. The Society believes, and once incorporated the thought in a resolution of the Board of Trustees, that it is better to make possible honorable and normal business practices at as reasonable a price as possible, than to give money outright and thus perhaps pauperize and weaken. This thought was propounded in 1910, in an era when rugged individualism was esteemed much more highly than now, and any efforts to alleviate the distress of the poor through government funding was regarded as downright communism. Whether or not you agree that this is a valid tenet, it can hardly be denied that it may be more comforting for the proud man, who needs a bottle of cough medicine for his child, to know that he can raise the price of it from the Provident by borrowing a dollar on his fountain pen, than to have to beg the druggist.

In other forms of lending, the lender holds notes against the borrower. A bank can bring suit or garnishee a co-signer; the wicked sheriff can foreclose the widow's mortgage and take over the house. But the Provident Loan Society has no such right of action if a borrower defaults on his loan; and through the Society's own influence upon small-loan legislation, this is true generally of all pawnbrokers as well. He must sell unclaimed collateral at public auction at the expiration of the loan's term, which is for a period of one year. The Provident sends a warning notice just before this time, and never sells the collateral before another grace period of a further three or four months. That enables sending an additional three or four warnings. If there is no reply, then and then only does an article go up on the auction block.

This practice isn't completely out of consideration for the borrower, although in the case of the Society that is the main reason. The simple fact is that, originally at its own initiative, the Provident created what is now the law. A pawnbroker must pay back to the borrower any surplus realized at the auction sale over and above the amount of the loan and accrued interest! Think about that. A $100 loan on a ring that only realizes $80 at public auction shows a $20 loss on the principal, plus loss of the interest that should have been collected. But a $100 loan that brings $1,000 at sale—and this, as you will find out, is by no means a wild or even particularly unusual occurrence—means that the Provident gets repaid its $100 plus interest, but the surplus of nearly $900 is paid to the borrower! Over the years, the Society has returned to borrowers millions of dollars of excess receipts from the auction sales of their collateral. Some have actually made loans with the full intention never to redeem their goods, but to let them go to sale eventually. At least they know that a sure market exists at the Society's auction sales. So the sales can produce nothing but a loss for the Society. Articles that fetch good prices do nothing more than repay the outstanding loan with its proper interest; articles that bring disappointing prices produce losses, often serious ones. It's clear why a number of warning notices to borrowers about impending sales of their property is a good idea for the Society, as well as a service to the borrower

You may well wonder how the institution could even have survived, let alone prosper, with such an altruistic policy. The answer is that only a very small percentage of loans are permitted to go to sale by the borrowers. In normal times, only 1 or 2 percent are not redeemed, or renewed for another year by the payment of the interest charge. During serious business depressions the percentage rises, but even at the depths of the Depression it never came to more than about 8 percent. So the Society's losses on the sales have been much more than compensated by the collection of interest on that overwhelming percentage of loans that are redeemed, renewed, or bring a sale price that clears the principal and interest.

The anecdotes and even legends that surround the auction sales, ranging from the humorous and pathetic to the fantastic and dramatic, deserve their own full treatment in a later part of this book. Here, in the general description of the Provident's benevolent stance, it is sufficient to note that the sales are conducted completely for the borrower's benefit insofar as any profit is concerned.

On March 17, 1939, forty-five years after its founding, when The Provident Loan Society had expanded to become the largest lending organization in the world in its field, *The New York Times* ran another editorial that read in part: "This is not a charitable institution. It is a self-sustaining agency to support a public need. Its management is in the hands of trustees who are men of large affairs with philanthropic interests, giving of their time and thought without compensation. Its one purpose is to make it possible for people in need to borrow money at the lowest rate consistent with sound business principles. It pays its way and has in doing so accomplished a service that could not have been rendered by a purely commercial management, on the one hand, or by continuous reliance for support, on the other hand, by philanthropy. Here is an instance of a business maligned and ridiculed through the centuries which has been lifted to a level of high service to this community and which has furnished a model to many other cities."

In the light of the financial era in which it was established, and that of the great Depression years in which it grew to its peak eminence, The Provident Loan Society was truly an unselfish community service, absolutely unique in dedication to its mission, incorruptible in its methods. If this were not true, it would be hard to believe that of the fifteen distinguished citizens who formed its original Board of Trustees, eleven died in office and the other four retired for personal reasons that had nothing to do with disenchantment with their trusteeship. What is more, continued service to the Society seems to be a responsibility that passed from one generation to the next, either through family or through business partnerships. Jacob H. Schiff and Solomon Loeb, his father-in-law and business partner, were incorporators and original contributors. When Solomon Loeb died, his grandson, Mortimer Schiff, succeeded him and was in turn succeeded by his son, John M. Schiff. In the house of Morgan, J. P. Morgan, Sr., was an incorporator and original contributor. J. P. Morgan, Jr., was later a member; Dwight Morrow and Russell C. Leffingwell, Morgan partners, became trustees. Joseph Milbank saw his son, Jeremiah Milbank, become a trustee. V. Everit Macy served as a trustee for over a quarter of a century, and his son, Valentine E. Macy, became a member. Cornelius Vanderbilt, Jr., was elected to the Board after the death of his father, one of the first trustees. And the same is true of the Sloanes, the Tods, the Jenningses, the Bakers, and the deForests.

It has been a noble tradition and one I still find rather stirring today, in a climate where being a Morgan partner or a private philanthropist doesn't seem all that good or wonderful a thing as it once did.

When was "once"? Well, for me it was one very early morning when I timidly but hopefully walked into the front door of the Executive Office at what will always be 346 Fourth Avenue for me (although the real estate lobby has long since ludicrously renamed it Park Avenue South). I was fresh out of college but with no money and no job, looking for work—any sort of work—at the very bottom of the Depression. I certainly had no thoughts about becoming a Morgan partner, but I did desperately want the job at the Provident that I had heard existed. What twenty-one-year-old young man wouldn't at that moment of financial desperation? Something like half of all one's friends, each with a college diploma tucked away on an upper closet shelf, were unable to find any job at all if there was no Daddy's business to go into. Many had tried to become insurance salesmen, or were walking around town trying to sell something else. But salesmen live on commissions from their sales, and in 1932 very few people had the money to buy anything substantial enough to throw off a decent commission. For most who tried door-to-door selling, it became apparent very quickly that nothing much was ever going to come out of this sort of work, and a fundamental extra problem was how to keep up morale at home by maintaining some sort of pretense that one had a job. To do that, you had to leave the house or apartment some time in the early morning and not return until late afternoon. Even if you weren't going to make any money, there remained those hours to kill. For many, the cheap matinee movie houses became a way of life, for while admission was fifteen cents in many of them, and practically never more than twenty-five cents, you could do without dessert and coffee at lunch at the Automat and break even on your frugal budget. As one of my friends put it one evening when I asked him what sort of day he had had, "I was one of this nation's distinguished commercial ambassadors who represented us at the cinema palaces."

Even a double-feature at one of the numerous West 42nd Street cheap movie houses wasn't enough to fill up the long hours of what the home folk would regard as your working day, but an instructive, entertaining, and inexpensive hour could always be passed after the movies at Hubert's Museum, also on that same 42nd Street block between Broadway and 8th Avenue. Hubert's is still there, but only as a penny arcade sort of place, with pinball machines and peep shows. Those attractions existed on the street-level floor back in the days of which I write, but each one cost an extra penny or nickel on top of the general admission price, which meant we were not prone to splurge on them too often.

But what wonders were spread before your eyes in the museum itself, located on the basement floor below the street! Your ten-cents admission was the total charge to roam at will, and for as long as you liked. The Past Great held court there, each enthroned on his or her separate throne, nodding and talking to all of us who came in out of the rain, signing autographs. There were holdovers from the circus, such as Tiny Tim, the World's Smallest Man, and The Tattooed Lady, more of whose anatomy was exposed than any female at a burlesque show. Even more interesting to a sports fan like myself, if even more pathetic, was the sight of two ancient sports immortals, passing their final days being viewed by the rubbernecks and being nice to them. One was Grover Cleveland Alexander, everyone's nominee as belonging on any all-time all-star baseball team selection, who only half a dozen years before had thrilled the nation in what was to be his baseball swan song. In 1926, when he was old as baseball players go and obviously near the end of his long career, an inveterate hard drinker whose taste for the hard stuff hadn't waned with the passing years, he was fired by the Chicago Cubs in midseason and picked up as a kind of desperate gamble by the St. Louis Cardinals. They were fighting for the National League pennant and needed an extra pitcher who might conceivably help out now and then in the stretch drive. The Cardinals not only did win the pennant but, in the World Series against the greatest of baseball teams, the

New York Yankees of that era when Babe Ruth and Lou Gehrig were at their peak, won the final and deciding game, 3–2, on the strength of Alexander's incredible heroics.

Alex had already done what seemed to be the impossible. He had won two games of the Series prior to this last deciding one, and the previous day he had gone the full nine innings. He was certainly entitled to sit in the bullpen and take his ease, but in the seventh inning of that last game, with the score 3–2 against them, the Yankees filled the bases with two out. And the great young slugger Tony Lazzeri was coming to bat.

Rogers Hornsby, the Cardinal manager, gave walking papers to his pitcher, Jesse Haines, and signaled to the bullpen. Out waddled Old Alex to take up this new burden. The rest is history. Lazzeri struck out swinging, and only six more Yankees managed to face Alexander in the final two innings, as he held onto the slim lead and won the game and the championship for the Cardinals. If it had been election time, he certainly could have been elected mayor of St. Louis that night. And so warm and sentimental was the country's feeling that he might even have made it to the Presidency. At that, he might not have been any worse than some.

But now, here he was sitting up on a podium in Hubert's Museum, saying very little but nodding and smiling a little at the kids. Heaven knows what sort of money he got for doing this, but I suppose it was enough to keep some sort of roof over his head, and a steady supply of cheap gin, and that was all that Alex ever really asked of the world.

In another corner, on a similar dais, sat Jack Johnson, the former heavyweight prizefighting champion of the world and the first black man ever to achieve that title. Johnson boxed professionally for twenty-nine years and had 109 major fights, and wore the heavyweight crown from 1907 to 1915. He is said to have made between half a million and a million dollars over that period—which of course, without any meaningful income tax assessment then, would be equivalent to many millions today. But Johnson was a high liver and spent it all a lot faster than he made it. He turned to wrestling in Paris, tried bullfighting in Spain, and even once played the part of a general in the opera *Aïda* in New York, but he finished up on a chair in Hubert's Museum.

All of this was fascinating, if somewhat macabre, but the real high spot of Hubert's was its Flea Circus. Some anonymous genius had trained a troupe of performing *fleas* to put on a series of acts worthy of Ringling Brothers. The stage was a circular clean white platform set a few feet below the circular wall and railing that enclosed it, so spectators could look down upon what was going on. A large magnifying glass was passed around among them, so that intermittently each viewer could get a closer look at the details of costumes and performances. Costumes? Yes, indeed. Although I've never had the privilege of measuring a flea, he (or she) can't be even as big as an eighth of an inch, but each flea was caparisoned in rainbow dress besides which Solomon, in all his glory, would appear drab. Tiny little jackets, hoop skirts, infinitesimal hats, canes, *everything!* In one act, jinrikishas containing elegantly dressed Japanese flea ladies, each carrying a gay parasol, were pulled around in formation by rikisha-boy fleas. In another, a laboring flea plodded clockwise turning a carousel on which festive fleas were riding. And in a third, and surely the greatest act, two flea teams competed against each other in a soccer match, taking turns at kicking the tiniest of gossamer-weight balls!

Where are the fleas of yesteryear? Gone forever, I'm afraid, for the present manager of Hubert's tells me that the one mad genius who trained them and put on the show, and whose name he can't even remember, retired to New Orleans many years ago and died there. There must be a lot of us, who were jobless in the early Thirties and had the empty days to fill, who are grateful to him.

Still, now and then an honest-to-God job that paid an actual weekly salary in cash in a small manila pay envelope did emerge. It practically never showed up in the almost non-existent "Help Wanted" columns, but usually through the grapevine and a tip from a friend. That was what happened to me. I had unsuccessfully been looking for a job for some months after getting out of Princeton, and had even taken a brief pathetic stab at selling life insurance. The most significant end result had been that I had seen a lot of movies.

Then one day a friend of my father's, Leon Henderson, who soon afterward became the chief administrator of Roosevelt's National Recovery Act (NRA) program, told me that if I were interested he thought he could get me a job with The Provident Loan Society of New York. Leon was at that time associated with the Department of Remedial Loans of the Russell Sage Foundation, which in turn was closely connected to the Charity Organization Society, so his word carried a lot of clout when a big opportunity like this opened up! It sounded great. I was to be a clerk of some sort, and although I had majored in English literature at college, that sounded okay. Mathematics had always been one of my better subjects, and I could be effectively methodical and accurate. The hours were just about as good as any office worker enjoyed (enjoyed?) in 1932. Check in at the office by 8:45 each weekday—and that did *not* mean 8:46—and leave at 5:15 (*not* 5:14). On Saturdays, 8:45 to 12:15. You were permitted Sundays off for gracious living.

Admittedly, the starting salary was not quite up to what I might have hoped for in view of the beginning rate some college men were achieving. Many of my friends who had landed real jobs were making $20 a week. (One of them, when I asked what he made, told me that his salary ran into *four* figures—and stopped abruptly. For the less mathematically inclined of my readers, fifty-two weeks at $20 a week comes to $1,020.) But the Provident Loan was a conservative, nonprofit institution, and they could only start me at $16 a week. Still, the opportunity for advancement was there, and I could look forward to making $20 within a year or so, if I made good. And kept my nose clean.

I was in no position to dicker.

CHAPTER 2

The Aspirin Age and Me

Eager beaver that I was, I tried conscientiously to find out everything I could about this strange business into which chance had landed me, for I had never heard of it before. I was by no means alone in my ignorance. Although approximately half a million New Yorkers were availing themselves each year during the Depression of the Provident's services, and the actual number of transactions were as many as a million and a half, millions of other people had no idea, or merely the vaguest notion, of the Society's unique qualities, goals, and methods.

For about a month I didn't learn too much, for my only contact was the very elderly boss of the mail room. During the Depression, subsequently labeled "The Aspirin Age" in Isabel Leighton's brilliant symposium, one of the causes of young men's headaches was the fact that new employees were invariably hazed for a while after they were hired. This tradition was born in the English public schools and perpetuated in basic training in the U.S. Army, as I was to learn ten years later. It had as its avowed purpose cutting the props out from under the overly egotistic and bringing them down to realistic earth. Dr. Freud would have given it a different label—sadism—and I suspect Dr. Freud would have been right.

In any event, for a month I ran errands, tied packages, and did other inspiring jobs such as going around the Executive Office first thing every morning with a tray bearing a large bottle of ink and a chamois cloth to fill each of the desk fountain pens and wipe its nib to a glowing polish. If I had time to ask my supervisor in the mail room any questions about the Provident, he didn't know any answers except how many desk fountain pens there were. (There were a lot. The ball-point pen wasn't invented until years later.)

But Leon Henderson, God bless him, had been asking his particular friend at the Society, E. Munroe Bates, about me. Bates, a Senior Vice President, not only created a statistical clerk's job for me (with a desk fountain pen of my very own that someone else subsequently filled and wiped clean every morning) but took me under his wing as his personal assistant. Munroe was the most intelligent and kindest of men, and my subsequent close association with him for a decade is one of my happiest and most rewarding business memories. From the very first day, he not only knew all the answers to my questions but expanded upon them with anecdotes.

The stock reply to the question, "What sort of collateral will the Society make a loan upon?" is: "Any personal property not too bulky, fragile, or perishable to be stored in its vaults, if it has an established market value at auction in New York City and is owned by the pledger without liens or encumbrances." That's pretty clear. And it answers, but makes no less interesting, the sort of inquiries that Munroe told me were constantly being asked of Provident appraisers in person, by mail, and by telephone:

"Can you make me a loan on a group of live chinchillas?"

"I have a factory full of new sewing machines. How much can I get on them?"

"An oil well is being drilled on my property and I need a couple of thousand dollars now in anticipation of the royalties I'll be receiving. Can you accommodate me?"

Clearly the answers all had to be "No" on such requests as these. With all its goodwill and desire to help any and every segment of society, the Provident Loan has its limitations, as expressed in the formula reply that bars all loans on livestock, furniture, factory equipment, china, glassware, most objects of art, and real estate. Additionally, loans cannot be made on intangibles of uncertain value, such as stocks, bonds, mortgages, or evidences of debt owed to the prospective pledger.

This means that practically all loans are made on comparatively small objects of some, and oftentime great, value. Precious-stone jewelry accounts for most of the larger loans, and in this category diamond jewelry dominates overwhelmingly. All Provident Loan appraisers in every office are qualified to make diamond loans. On other precious stones—emeralds, sapphires, rubies—and on pearls, a specialist's expertise is needed, and the pledger is sent to an office that can handle such collateral. Loans are made on really good semiprecious jewelry too, but it has to be an article set in precious metal, such as is sold in a retail jewelry shop. Since the value of semiprecious stones varies so widely and unaccountably according to fashions and whims of the moment, very little consideration is given to the stone's value, and such a loan is more likely to be predicated upon the value of the setting.

Costume jewelry, no matter how pretty, and that Indian bracelet you picked up while changing trains at the Albuquerque railroad station (unless set in sterling silver) won't rate even a minimum loan.

Gold articles such as old-fashioned chains and watches constitute a great percentage of loans. Once again, the size of a loan is based almost completely upon the article's breakup or assay value, although some consideration is given to desirability and sales appeal on a particularly attractive piece. But not much, because this is a value that has to be a personal estimate, and the general run of the Society's appraisers are not trained for that. They deal in the meat-and-potatoes part of jewelry evaluation: If a pledger's article seems to require a connoisseur's evaluation, he is sent to an office that houses a specialist.

All this means that a borrower approaching the Provident for the first time is often surprised and shocked at the low pledge value the appraiser gives his collateral. He does not realize that what he paid for it in a retail establishment bears very little direct relationship to the loan the Society is able to extend. If and when the Provident ever has to sell his article at public auction, in case he doesn't redeem it, the sale will be made at something very close to the price that wholesale jewelers would pay for it. The markup from a wholesale price to that set in a retail establishment is an extremely high one in the jewelry field, almost invariably 100 percent and often 200 percent or more in one of the elegant Fifth Avenue establishments. On top of that, a retail purchase involves a luxury tax and a city tax. Additionally, the Society has to allow for the interest that would accumulate up to the time of sale, and the cost of sale. Finally, it has to be conservative in making loans, in view of the depreciation that well may take place in the market over the more than a year between the time of the loan and the time the article may possibly have to go to sale.

So it's likely to turn out that a person who has paid, let us say, $500 for a diamond ring may find that all The Provident Loan Society will lend on it is $150. That isn't a denigration of his ring, or an implication that the retail jeweler fleeced him. Such a proportion is closer to the rule than the exception, for the reasons just detailed. If all he needs for the moment is the $150, and he is going to redeem the ring eventually anyhow, all is well. He gets his loan, and when he reclaims the ring he will only be paying a minimum interest charge. Meanwhile, the ring is stored better and more safely than in a jewelry case in a bureau drawer. But if things continue to be difficult for him and he chooses not to redeem, the Provident Loan's auction sales automatically offer an opportunity to sell the piece and get him at least as good a price for it as he would be likely to get offering it himself to a wholesale jeweler. After all, these sales are highly competitive, with jewelers and private individuals bidding against each other, so the level of prices invariably is at, and often is above, wholesale level. And if the ring goes to sale and fetches $400—a figure perhaps closer to what the pledger unrealistically thought he might get at the time he made the loan— almost all of the $250 surplus between his $150 loan and the $400 realized will be paid to him, not retained by the Society.

Silverware is another large category upon which the Provident makes loans. Dealers' and collectors' items, such as coins and unused sheets of U.S. stamps of value, are legitimate collateral but require the pledger to visit the office that has a specialist in judging them. A variety of other readily salable items justify a Provident loan: cameras, binoculars and field glasses, typewriters, and the like. Loans were once made on furs, but that policy has been discontinued for reasons that will be explained.

Munroe Bates proceeded with my basic education even though I was as yet not concerned with most of this because, as his assistant in the Executive Office, I had no direct connection either with the branch offices that were making the loans or with the Auction Sales department that sold unredeemed collateral. Later I had a lot to do with both, particularly the latter.

"Mr. Bates, what kind of person makes pledge loans?" (A parenthetical note: In those days at least, and I would suspect even now, no one—but no one—addressed fellow workers by first names unless they were exactly on the same level of position. I dated a girl in the office for several years but we were always "Miss M." and "Mr. S." to each other between 8:45 and 5:15. Munroe Bates became a close enough friend that he is godfather to one of my children, but it wasn't until I reached the rank of becoming an officer of the Society that we could be on a "Munroe—Peter" basis.)

So . . . "Mr. Bates, what kind of person makes pledge loans?"

The answer was that just about anyone, from every walk of life, was likely to do so. That is why the loans varied from many in the thousands of dollars to the more normal average loan that represented something like a week's salary in The Aspirin Age—$50 to $80—and then all the way down to the $1 loan for a meal that day.

Theodore Dreiser, in his later years, had no hesitation in

telling about the assistance he sought and obtained from the Society in his early days. In an interview with Robert Van Gelder in *The New York Times* Book Section in March 1941, he told of living in a $1.50-a-week room in Williamsburg, Brooklyn, where he could no longer pay his rent. A public charity organization refused assistance, so he had to give up his room. When he left it he had only 15 cents left to his name. He did have a watch, and he took it to a branch office of the Provident Loan.

"The clerk seemed hardly to look at me . . . he put the glass in his eye and examined the watch. Well, I hadn't eaten in a long time and was sick. I was thinking perhaps he would give me a dollar, but I warned myself 'Don't count on more than 50 cents.' After looking at the watch, the clerk asked for my name and address. I had to explain I had no address at the moment. Then he pushed the paper [the ticket] over to me. It was marked $25. It was hard for me to speak. 'This,' I said, 'This is for $25.' 'I know it,' he said, 'come in and get your watch back when you can.'

"Imagine! I bought a pair of shoes for $2. The shoes I'd had were very far gone. And my hat had blown off in a subway. I bought a hat. A room at the Mills Hotel—25 cents a night. I felt a slight return of confidence. I needed an outdoor job, a job as a laborer, anything that would give me a chance to work and be self supporting." Shortly thereafter, Mr. Dreiser continued, he did get a laborer's job and saved enough so that nine months later he could resume his chosen career of writing. It's quite possible that without The Provident Loan Society, *An American Tragedy* would never have been written.

At the other end of the pendulum, in the area of large

loans, perhaps no single one was solicited for more dramatic purposes than the $50,000 that Mrs. Evalyn Walsh McLean wanted to borrow in the spring of 1932.

Mrs. McLean was the heiress owner of the Washington *Star* and a not infrequent patron of The Provident Loan Society whenever her newspaper needed additional financing. The amounts of the loans she required invariably were of a size that demanded very spectacular collateral, and Mrs. Mc-Lean was certainly the lady who could furnish it. Her jewels were many and magnificent, and among them was the fabulous Hope diamond, a completely unique stone, approximately 44.5 carats in size and so blue in color as almost to resemble a cornflower-blue sapphire rather than a diamond. Its color is the basic reason why the Hope has always been so esteemed, but a secondary appeal lies in its unusually dramatic and frequently unfortunate history. Originally it is said to have been stolen from a Burmese temple, where it had formed the eye of an idol. Louis XIV purchased it in 1669 from the great French traveler Tavernier, and Louis XVI gave it to Marie Antoinette, who, as you will recall, didn't come to the happiest of ends. It is probably along about here that the diamond picked up its reputation as being a stone surrounded by misfortune. Later, what we now know as the Hope diamond, which is only a large portion of the original stone, turned up successively in Amsterdam and the Spanish court, and eventually was bought by the London banker Henry Thomas Hope, a relative of the Duke of Newcastle. It then received the name by which it has been known ever since, the Hope diamond. There were several subsequent possessors, for if the unlucky association with the stone had no other aspect than financial reversals for its owners, that invariably seemed to be the case. The third generation Lord Hope wasted his fortune and died in poverty. Abdul Hamid II, of Turkey, came into possession of the diamond later and was overthrown in a revolution. Finally the gem traveled to Cartier, in Paris, and it was there in 1911 that Edward Beale McLean bought it for his wife. Once again major tragedy struck—the McLean's son was killed almost immediately after the purchase.

Two decades passed with the Hope in Mrs. McLean's possession and no further catastrophes, but on that day in 1932 Mrs. McLean's request for a $50,000 loan was infinitely more frantic than at any time she had ever approached the Society before or since. Not only did the Provident have to make the loan *instantly,* but also in cash of relatively small-denomination bills. She needed the money to pay the ransom demanded by the person claiming that he was the kidnapper of Charles Augustus Lindbergh's infant son! She wanted to pledge the diamond that had the tragic reputation in order to spare the country's hero and his wife an even greater tragedy.

Few of the many traumas that blanketed the nation during The Aspirin Age were more tormenting to so many people as the kidnapping of Charles, first-born to America's idol of the time and his lovely, talented wife, Anne Morrow Lindbergh (who was, incidentally, the daughter of Dwight Morrow, one of the founders of The Provident Loan Society). Five years earlier, through the night of May 20, 1927, and into the evening of the next day, Lindbergh had flown his small monoplane, *The Spirit of St. Louis,* across the 3,600 miles from Curtis Field in Long Island to Paris in thirty-three and a half hours. It was the first solo nonstop flight across the Atlantic, and despite Lindbergh's shyness and many attempts to escape notoriety, he and his many subsequent feats were constantly in the news, always with admiration. There were no Lindbergh detractors then, for this was many years before his involvement with politics and his widely broadcast military opinions at the outset of World War II (convinced of the superiority of the Nazi forces, he became a leading spokesman for the America First isolationist group, and lost much of his popularity).

But in March 1932 Lucky Lindy was unquestionably the country's Golden Boy, and when the shocking news burst out over the radio waves and screamed across the front-page headlines that his son had been kidnapped from the Lindbergh home in Hopewell, New Jersey, the country went into shock. There followed a whole series of desperate searches, attempts to make contact with the kidnappers, prayers, and eventual deep mourning when the baby's body was finally discovered some time after ransom money had been paid. That ransom money was probably paid to the real kidnapper, Bruno Richard Hauptmann, who was tried, convicted, and executed on the basis of very convincing circumstantial evidence, a part of which was his possession of some of the marked ransom money. Until the very end Hauptmann maintained that he was innocent, but almost everyone was convinced of his guilt.

Prior to paying this ransom and the final grim discovery of the baby's body, a number of false leads and misinformation had sent Federal authorities off on unproductive trails, but none was more cruel to the Lindberghs and the stricken nation than the hoax perpetrated upon Evalyn Walsh McLean by one Gaston B. Means. This swindler got in touch with Mrs. McLean and told her that he had been chosen by the kidnapper(s) as the intermediary between them and anyone rich enough to pay the ransom demanded for the child. Mrs. McLean had been picked as a likely candidate, Means said, and since it later developed that he was acting alone, with no knowledge of who the kidnappers might be, he picked well. For Mrs. McLean assured him that she would come up with the $50,000 that Means said was needed. Mrs. McLean turned to The Provident Loan Society once again, offering the Hope Diamond as security. She undoubtedly felt that it was her most valuable gem and that there couldn't possibly be any hesitation on the Society's part in tendering a loan that was so small a proportion of its worth. (As a matter of interest, the specific price that the Hope diamond might bring over the last half century is not a matter of public record. When Mrs. McLean died in 1947, the diamond was sold along with her other jewels to the New York jewelry merchant, Harry Winston, for a total sum said to be in the neighborhood of $1.5 million, but what proportion of that was attributable to the Hope was not revealed. Without question, however, it must have been a very sizable one.)

Mrs. McLean did not come to New York herself on this mission but sent her authorized agent. He seemed somewhat surprised, although not completely stunned, when the Provident's executives, who were considering the situation, seemed a trifle reluctant to make the loan on the Hope. Mrs. McLean was a very sophisticated person about diamonds and about the Society's methods, and she may well have anticipated the reaction and prepared her agent for it.

The trouble with accepting the Hope diamond as collateral was the possibility, even if it was remote, that it might not be redeemed by Mrs. McLean and would have to be put on the auction block a year later. Remember that this was in the depths of the Depression. What prospective purchaser would be likely to be in the Provident's auction sale audience if that day ever came? And what competitive bidders to assure a proper sales price? The Maharajah of Punjab? The Richard Burton and Elizabeth Taylor of that day, whoever they may have been? The Keeper of the Crown Jewels of England? It's quite true that one or more of this type of bidder might attend if the sale were advertised and promoted sufficiently in advance. But, on the whole, the only regular and solid patrons the Society could count on were the wholesale jewelry dealers from the Bowery and from West 47th Street, for whom the purchase of a single diamond solitaire, with a price running even into four figures, was a major investment. If some of them did happen to want to plunge on so spectacular a purchase, they would undoubtedly pool their resources and form a combination, and in that event who possibly would compete with them and establish any bidding? Nor could the alternative gamble, usually available to speculators buying huge diamonds, be considered—that of cutting the stone up into a number of smaller, more easily salable gems. The Hope's value and unique attraction repose in the form in which it exists, and of all stones in the world this is the least likely candidate for anyone even to dream of cutting up into smaller stones.

The Society's executives and appraisers brooded over the problem and explained it to Mrs. McLean's representative. Armed by her to anticipate their problems, he reached into another pocket and produced another diamond, more than three times as large and a pure flawless fine white! While it had no such fabulous reputation as the Hope diamond, it was quite a spectacular little secondary trinket as additional or substitute collateral. No puny little 44-carat diamond with a diameter about the size of an elongated oval quarter, as was the Hope. No, this one weighed over 140 carats, was named the Star of the East, and looked nearer the size of a walnut.

From the Provident's standpoint, this was an infinitely safer risk—assuming, as never turned out to be the case, any risk existed at all, for Mrs. McLean always redeemed her jewelry within a short period. But *if* the Society had ever been forced to put the Star up for auction, unquestionably a number of dealer combinations would have been interested and would have competed against each other for it. Even if no one single buyer could be found, the Star would have been ideal for cutting up into a substantial number of marvelous, eminently salable smaller gemstones ranging, let us say, from 2 to 10 carats each.

The Hope diamond was in our office on this occasion, and those of us who were fortunate enough to be present saw it, held it in our hands, and examined it. But it was never used as a pledge for a loan. Instead, the Star became Mrs. McLean's collateral, and the Provident Loan came up with her $50,000. She turned the money over to Gaston Means—and never saw it again. Despite Means's insistence at the time that he too had been bilked, and had given the money to the "kidnapper," it seems virtually certain that his story had been a brutal fabrication to fleece Mrs. McLean.

Mrs. McLean suffered the loss but won the nation's sympathy and admiration for her attempt. Soon afterwards, as always whenever she borrowed money for the financial difficulties the Washington *Star* was running into, she redeemed her diamond. Apparently she invariably could scrape up the $50,000 or so she needed to redeem her jewelry out of what was tucked away in the sugar bowl in her kitchen, but when she couldn't put her hands on the sugar bowl and was in a hurry, she turned to the Provident. The fact that she reclaimed her diamond means the Society might just as well have accepted the Hope diamond rather than the Star. In that case, still another chapter in the romantic if unhappy legend of the Hope would have been written. Actually, it has now settled down into a happy retirement. Some time after Harry Winston bought it, he presented it to the United States Government, which keeps it on display at the Smithsonian Institution. If it still retains its fabled aura of dire fate for the owner, you may be glad if your political opponents are in power.

CHAPTER 3

The Borrowers' Tales

It should be noted here that the last story, like many others that will follow, could not be told when they happened, or for years afterwards. Obviously The Provident Loan Society was the embodiment of circumspectness, and regarded all its dealings as privileged communications. None of us would even have thought of telling tales out of school as long as it might conceivably have hurt or embarrassed the pledger, who was entitled to his or her complete privacy. If anyone had done so, he would have been clearly and flagrantly breaching a confidence and would have been fired before even trying to offer an explanation. For there could be no justifiable explanation.

But just as is the case in law with respect to libel, or invasion of privacy, the rules are understandably called off when a person dies. One cannot libel the dead, one need not respect a dead person's privacy, and history is made to be recorded. Almost all the episodes recounted in this book are about people no longer living; in the few cases where that is not the case, names are not revealed. In Evalyn Walsh Mc-

Lean's case there is still another reason why confidentiality is not required. She had absolutely no reserve while she was alive about telling of her dealings with The Provident Loan Society, and even wrote about them herself.

It may well come as a surprise that Mrs. McLean's representative just wandered up to New York from Washington with the Hope diamond in one pocket and the Star of the East in another. Surely that's not the way to transport two of the most famous and valuable gem diamonds in the world! Hadn't the armored car been invented in 1932?

Yes, it had. But the armored car, which is necessary for transporting heavy or bulky valuables such as gold bars or a huge amount of cash, is considered a very poor way of shipping small, light articles of immense value, such as these two diamonds. An armored car is an obvious target for a holdup, even if a robbery is difficult to effect. It carries an unwritten label that something very important and expensive is inside it.

That is why knowledgeable diamond people never avail themselves of this service. It has been found through the years that the second best way to send a diamond from one place to the other is by personal courier, if that's practical. Ordinary registered mail is even better, insured for some small sum like $5 or $10.

Even in these days, when the mails are not as dependable as they once were, insured registered mail is handled with care and respect. The recipient has to be sought out personally and must sign a receipt. If that doesn't take place for one reason or another, the package is returned to the sender with the same precautions. If one is mailing a valuable diamond, a very big insurance valuation should not be put upon the package for the same reason that makes the armored car a poor idea—it instantly pinpoints the package as a possible target for robbery. A small insurance coverage guarantees the same special care in delivery as would a large one.

While insured registered mail is the best recourse, the personal and unostentatious hand delivery is next best and is used sometimes, usually because swift action is called for (as in the case of Mrs. McLean's mission). The rules are: Don't pick a person whose appearance, dress, or position would make him or her a likely target possibility, even if not carrying something extremely valuable. In other words, don't choose anyone like either Bebe Rebozo or Jackie Onassis as your messenger. And don't let anyone, other than the carrier and the recipient, know that the package is going to be hand-delivered. (I assure you that all this is more difficult and riskier than using registered mail.)

Mrs. McLean's representative, completely and justifiably trusted by her for years, was dim of facial appearance and so modestly dressed that he would have been lost in a crowd of welfare applicants. His only concern was that he not have a hole in the pockets in which he carried the Hope and the Star.

I was almost a brand-new young employee of the Society at the time, and certainly no principal in the affair. It merely was my good fortune to be present while the Hope and the Star were being displayed, as the result of Munroe Bates having taken me into his office with him. As I consider the problem of how Mrs. McLean's agent got back to Washington equally unostentatiously, but this time having to carry $50,000 in small bills, I think he must not have had to do so. More probably the Provident issued a check and made arrangements with a Washington bank to honor it immediately in the way requested.

Some very few years later I did get involved myself with Mrs. McLean and her pledges. She had given us the Star again as security for whatever she needed at the time for her newspaper's use, and now not only wanted to redeem it but wanted to do so that afternoon so that she could wear it the same evening. By this time I was a veteran hired hand, highly enough placed as Mr. Bates's assistant to be completely trust-worthy, and certainly dim and inconspicuous enough in my $15 suit from Barney's and my horn-rimmed glasses to be just as lost in a crowd as the agent had been. I was told to take the Star out of our vaults, go to Washington, and return it to Mrs. McLean at her home, *Friendship*. I was to pick up her receipt and her check, and be damned sure not to lose either before I could turn them in to the office the next day.

I could not be expected to finance this expensive expedi-tion myself, obviously, even though by that time I must have been making as much as perhaps $40 or $50 a week. This was years before expense accounts and credit cards, and even if it had not been, The Provident Loan Society wasn't the sort of organization to countenance irresponsible things like those. So I was told to make out a petty cash voucher for my re-quirements for the trip, then make an exact accounting justi-fying whatever I had to spend after my return.

It is difficult today to conceive how exact and meticulous all decent and responsible employees were expected to act in money matters in those days. If it was true generally, nowhere was such thinking held in greater honor than at the Provi-dent. One personal experience occurred when I had been temporarily assigned to a branch office for experience in that area of operations. The office closed to the public at 4:30, and balancing the day's business and the cash on hand was invariably accomplished well before 5 o'clock, when we could leave. But that day the cash was 8 cents out! Horrors! No panic, but also no question that *everyone,* from the office manager to the porter, had to stay until the two balanced. Absolutely useless for someone like myself to say, "Damn it! I've got a date. Here's 8 cents—toss it into the till!"

As I recall, my date and I missed dinner and grabbed a couple of hot dogs between the first and second acts. She was not particularly pleased.

But I wander afield from my mission to Mrs. McLean and to Washington. I did indeed have to figure out how much money to draw from petty cash. The round-trip coach fare to Washington in those days was just over $11, and that would be very nearly my only expenditure, and certainly the costly one. It did not matter that I was bearing in my pocket a 140-carat gemstone worth hundreds of thousands of dollars. Organizations like ours, and employees like me, didn't take taxicabs. And why should they? A surface trolley or a subway fare was 5 cents (and they were as safe as anywhere else, which was safe) whereas a taxi to Penn Station, with a tip, would run as much as 50 cents. Why take a taxi?

Nor was this a business mission for which there need be any requirement to reimburse me for money spent on meals. I had to eat in any case, didn't I? If I were working in New York I'd probably be having my lunch for about 35 cents at a place like the Automat. There were Automats in Washington too, weren't there?

Transportation from Union Station in Washington to

Friendship and back might involve four fares—call it another possible 20 cents—but maybe not. Didn't they have free transfers in Washington, just as they did in New York?

A $15 voucher for petty cash was surely going to take care of what I was entitled to draw, with at least a couple of dollars left over for emergencies. And it did. The next day I made an expense accounting that totaled $11.90, and returned $3.10 to the drawer. The only person I told about the fact that Mrs. McLean had invited me to lunch at *Friendship,* and stood me a delicious four-course meal—and wine with my meal!—was Munroe Bates. He would understand, appreciate, and condone. The basic notions of the Provident were such that someone other than Munroe might have suggested that, as a result of a business assignment, I had not found it necessary to buy my own lunch. Shouldn't I perhaps augment the Provident's petty cash drawer with the 35 cents I had saved?

Enough. I am teasing the Provident Loan's methods and attitudes of the 1930's past the point of fairness. Remember that these were hard times indeed and that all of us—employees, officers, and trustees alike—had been brought up in the "penny earned is a penny saved" tradition. I respected it myself and never questioned it. More to the point was the fact that the Society was a nonprofit institution, and no boss was lining his own pocket as the result of being mean or penurious to lesser workers.

Large loans, such as Mrs. McLean's, are isolated, spectacular, and dramatic occurrences in the Society's history, but they are no more fascinating than the throughout-the-year activity in small loans that the three Lower East Side branches conducted in my day—and large loans are much less important in the fulfillment of the Provident's goals to service the needy.

In the Depression years the Society was needed and used by the community more than it ever had been previously, or ever has been since. Twenty-two branch offices were spread all over New York: three in the Bronx, four in Brooklyn, and fifteen in Manhattan. Among the latter were three located in the then predominantly Jewish, poverty-stricken sector of the city known at the time as the Lower East Side (now the East Village). The offices were identified by the streets where they were located: Eldridge Street, Rivington Street, and East Houston Street. The streets are still there but the offices are not, for with the shift in ethnic populations over the past forty years, and with the civic need for The Provident Loan Society's services declining as easier credit has risen, they have been closed. Today only eight Provident Loan offices remain: one in Brooklyn; one in the Bronx; one in Jamaica, Long Island (remember?); and five in Manhattan. Quite intentionally and understandably, the ones that survive are those not located in the highest crime areas of the city. That consideration spelled the early demise of the three East Side offices, for the climate of the East Village today is certainly much more dangerous than it was in the 1930's.

Then it was essentially the home of the poorest people in New York. True to the Provident's charter, this meant that these three offices were constantly carrying out the Society's first aim, the lending of small amounts of money to the desperately needy, even at a loss. But the Lower East Side also was crowded with small-scale merchants who, while also very poor, were working hard to earn money. These were the pushcart peddlers who daily offered their wares in the streets and who seldom made enough of a profit to do more than live from week to week.

The Provident Loan was their bank, enabling them to finance their operations. Every Monday morning the doors of the East Side offices were opened to the impatient knocking of the peddlers, anxious to pledge their family's jewelry so they could set out buying the goods they hoped to sell over the next few days. Every Friday afternoon these same men, or some member of the family, would bring in their tickets to redeem the jewelry so that it could be worn with dignity over the weekend at social affairs and at religious services. The man of the family had sold the inventory that he had bought on Monday for enough of a profit to enable the family to survive. The principal of the loan had been recouped, and the Provident's interest charge for the intervening four days was miniscule, usually a matter of pennies. All was well until the next week, and the women could have their jewelry at the time it mattered.

Then, on the next Monday, diamond rings and gold bracelets were back in the man's hands and he was waiting, well before 9 o'clock in the morning, to secure a new loan for the new week's purchases.

It happens that the pushcart peddlers existed in such great numbers, formed so steady a weekly pattern of lending and repaying, that theirs is an outstanding example of the Provident's aid to those who have needed a small loan to tide them through times of crisis. But by no means have they been the only ones, in comparable situations, who found the Society an answer and a blessing. Thousands of small merchants with actual stores, manufacturers, contractors, the self-employed—people who from time to time required a loan to keep going until the next job came up—have turned to the Society for help and have not gone away empty-handed. As vaudeville was replaced by the movies, the silent movies by the talkies, the talkies by television, hundreds of people associated with the acting profession have hit barren stretches of nonemployment. A number of actors, including prominent stars, weathered the transition by bringing articles they had secured in prosperous days to a Provident Loan office, usually the one near Times Square.

One pledger, when he came back to an office to redeem the article on which the Society had made quite a substantial loan, told how the money had enabled him to save a million dollar piece of property from going to a mortgage holder. A formerly very wealthy European family pledged and repledged a few thousand dollars worth of their remaining family jewelry to reassemble various children and relatives in this country after the holocaust of World War II. Peoples of all nationalities, from lands all over the world, have sought and obtained loans for every variety of purpose and ambition, such as starting a farm in the Midwest; financing an education for themselves or their children; opening a new business in this, the country of their adoption; or sometimes just to assist fellow refugees who needed a start.

There is absolutely no clear definition of who is likely to turn to The Provident Loan Society in time of need or disaster. Sometimes their requirements are relieved by only a few dollars. But a man who must pay $25,000 to save his home, or else lose it in time of housing shortage, suffers "need" just as acutely as the woman who has lost her purse and has to pledge her wedding ring to get home.

The game of tennis has always been one of my passions, both as a player and as a spectator. As a boy, living on the south shore of Long Island, there was no year during the early to mid-1920's when I didn't make the ten-mile trip in order to see every day's play of the annual U.S. Tennis Championships at Forest Hills. During that stretch from 1920 through 1925, I never saw anyone win the men's singles championship other than the man generally acknowledged to have been the greatest player of all time, William Tatem Tilden II.

"Big Bill," the nickname that distinguished him from "Little Bill" Johnston, his greatest rival whom he invariably met and defeated in the final rounds, ruled the courts so completely during that six-year stretch that there truly was no other player who would ever beat him in an important match. In those six years he not only won our championship all six times but also won the Wimbledon crown on the two occasions he crossed the Atlantic to compete for it; and, representing the United States as our Number One singles player in the annual Davis Cup finals, he swept all twelve of his matches against the finest competition the world could produce.

The closest I had ever been able to come to him, as a hero-worshipping boy, was watching him play from court-side. The world spins on, however, and some twenty-five years later I not only met Tilden but worked with him. And, of all things, he had a story to tell about The Provident Loan Society.

I left the Provident in early 1942 to go into the Army in World War II, and when I came out at the end of 1945 I decided to accept an offer I had received to go into book publishing. Although I started out in the business end of the firm of Simon and Schuster, I soon showed more of a taste and aptitude for the editorial side and had gradually moved into it. Since sports books were one of my specialties, and Tilden's name, reputation, and even playing ability as he neared the age of sixty were still fantastic—in his fifties he pushed Bobby Riggs, then twenty-eight years old and the professional champion of the world, to the limit in a tournament match—I thought it would be great to get a book of tennis instruction from Tilden.

I got in touch with him, found him receptive to the idea, and set up an appointment. After a discussion and agreement about the book, which was published in 1950 under the title *How to Play Better Tennis* (and is still in print), the talk turned to more personal matters, and Bill asked me about myself.

When I told him of my first and only other job, with the Provident Loan, he grinned. Lighting a cigarette, he leaned back and started talking.

"Back in the early twenties, as you know, I won just about every tournament I ever entered, and I collected not only a mantelpiece but a closetful of silver trophies. So every time I was low on spending money, I gathered up a bag of them and hocked them at your old place—excuse me, 'pledged' them. The interest rates were cheaper than storage and you people kept very good care of them, stored them in vaults in flannel bags and even polished them now and then.

"Somehow I didn't patronize one office in particular, but

just brought in a batch of cups or trophies to whatever office happened to be convenient on that particular day. The result is that, at the time I'm referring to, I probably had outstanding loan tickets on four or five of the Provident's offices. Times Square, Grand Central, East 60th Street, Lenox Hill—heaven knows where. And each of the tickets simply said on it, '8 Silver Cups,' or '5 Silver Cups, 2 Silver Trays,' and so forth.

"One day I got a letter from the Germantown Cricket Club, which, as you will remember, was the site of one of the more important grass court tournaments preceding the Nationals at Forest Hills. It acknowledged my entry for that year and pointed out that I was in temporary possession of the permanent challenge bowl for the event. Each year the winner's name is inscribed upon it, but it is only kept for one year and then must be returned at the time of the next year's Germantown event so it can be presented to the next winner. Therefore, would I please be so kind as to return the trophy now, or at least bring it with me when I arrived for the tournament next week? Yours respectfully, etcetera, etcetera.

"Well, I couldn't find the damned thing anywhere around my place, and it was big enough that it couldn't have been hidden under my shirts in the drawer. I realized that it *must* be sitting in a Provident Loan vault, but which one? The loan tickets were of no value at all in telling me that.

"So I got on the phone and called your Executive Office and asked to speak to an officer. I forget the name of the man I got. He was no tennis bug and my name was only faintly recognizable to him, but he couldn't have been more cooperative and nicer if he had been you, with your interest in tennis.

On his instructions some four or five Provident offices spent a good part of the day opening their vaults, taking out my pieces, unwrapping and examining them to see if any one was the Germantown trophy, and then with one exception in one office, having to go through the whole thing backwards.

"But that one office did locate the bowl and got the word back to me that same day. So I was able to go there, pay off my loan and pick up the trophy, and take it down to Germantown a couple of days later with my honor intact. It would have been particularly embarrassing for me if I hadn't been able to do so, you know—more than any other tournament, because Germantown was my home town and all those people really knew me well enough to go after my scalp with tomahawks. I said a little prayer of thankfulness to the Provident Loan each night for some time afterwards."

Bill Tilden was only one of a great number of sports figures who found the Society a useful convenience. Some of them found it a place to cash in a prize that they didn't want to keep as much as they wanted some money. At worst they received the loan value and had no obligation to redeem the article. At best it would go to sale at the expiration of the loan period and toss off a surplus, which would mean more money for the borrower. It was by no means the worst way to sell one's trophies, and this was a time before professional sports had taken over so completely from amateur sports. Many athletes were very reluctant to give up their amateur status for a variety of reasons. Most major events were purely amateur, from the Olympic Games down. The opportunity to earn real money as a professional in almost any sport didn't even begin to compare with what is possible today. The result was that many amateurs kept that status officially, but covertly became "shamateurs," cashing in on their skills in whatever manner they could. Golfers and tennis players took out insurance licenses and would make their appearance at tournaments only if assured that they could sell a large policy. High school football players went to the college that would give them the best "student aid" in the form of a weekly salary for winding up an eight-day clock. And trophy winners made regular visits to a Provident Loan Society office.

One of the more interesting stories in this connection may well be apocryphal, for I never knew anyone who could vouch for it. Just the same, and more than once, I was told that back in 1912, after Jim Thorpe, the super-great college football hero from the Carlisle (Pa.) Indian Institute, won both the Olympic Games decathlon and the pentathlon at Stockholm, his two gold medals were pledged with the Society. No one would have paid any more or less attention to this than they would to any unusually interesting collateral, but in Thorpe's case a ruling subsequently came down from the Olympic Committee that he had to return the medals. Someone had unearthed the shattering revelation that prior to the Olympics, Thorpe had been paid to play baseball in the Eastern Carolina League in 1908 and 1909, which made him a professional ineligible to compete in the then supposedly simon-pure amateur Olympic Games. Thorpe did return the medals and, if the legend is true, had to redeem them first from the Provident Loan. In the record books, Hugo Wieslander of Sweden was thereinafter inscribed as the winner of the decathlon in that year, and Ferdinand Bie of Norway the pentathlon victor, but no one who is not Scandinavian remembers their names today, while Jim Thorpe is perhaps the most immortal of all American athletes.

There was one athletic prize that appeared so frequently at the same branch office, and was so recognizable, that the manager knew exactly what he could lend on it from previous experience, and didn't have to go through an involved new appraisal each time. Involved and complicated it would indeed have been, for it was the diamond-studded belt emblematic of the heavyweight wrestling championship of the world. It was perhaps the ugliest and most garish article ever fashioned, with the possible exception of the Crown Jewels of England, containing dozens of diamonds of extremely poor quality. But it all added up to a lot of carats, and many of the stones were extremely large. This meant it had a very substantial lending value, apart from any extra worth it might have for what it represented. (The extra value would be rated as zero by a Provident appraiser, although it might be considerable to a trophy collector. But who could count on a trophy collector being present at the auction sale if the belt ever had to be sold? That is why the appraiser had to base his loan upon nothing more than the breakup value of the diamonds as a wholesale dealer would view it, and this is the philosophy that forces many Provident offers on attractive or unusual articles to appear unduly conservative to the owner.)

The owner, in this case, was Stanislaus Zybysko, who ruled heavyweight wrestling for a very long stretch of time and who obviously found possession of the belt a great accommodation for being able to enjoy the little things of life. His circumstance obviously never became very desperate because he always redeemed his loans, and the belt never had to go to sale.

A great proportion of the sporting and theatrical fraternities were likely to patronize the Times Square branch office at 49th Street and Seventh Avenue—which of course isn't actually in Times Square at all, but just off it. As explained earlier, the Provident consciously picked its locations to be convenient to the center of things but not right in the heart of them, in order to spare shy pledgers embarrassment at being caught pawning the family jewels.

Branch office managers are vested with a great deal of authority and almost never have to seek advice or ask permission about making any loan. And of all managers at the time these next two stories took place, none ranked higher in the Society's confidence than the one at the Times Square office, Sol Glicksman. More about him later.

However, when a loan is requested for a very big amount, the pledger has to be referred to the Vice President at the Executive Office, who is in charge of the Appraisal Department. This is not so much because an experienced hand like Glicksman wouldn't be capable of establishing *bona fides,* or evaluating the article. It is more because the Provident's real purpose is to make smaller loans to as many people as require them, and not to strip its cash resources by making so many really large loans as might impede that goal.

A second factor is that such big loans usually involve comparatively lengthy sessions between the pledger and the Society's representative. The collateral is likely to be substantial, containing a number of precious stones, which means that the appraisal may take quite a while. Additionally, matters like proof of ownership must be conducted particularly carefully. The final reason is that the sort of person who is likely to own really outstanding and expensive pieces of jewelry, whether woman or man, appreciates and probably feels the need for a private office in which to conduct the transaction.

One such case seemed interesting enough at the time, but its full impact didn't register on us until months later. A well-dressed man appeared in the Times Square office looking for a large loan on a magnificent pair of star-sapphire cuff links. Three factors blocked the branch office from considering the loan. First, it was a larger sum request than the office was authorized to make. Second, the only appraisers capable of examining and setting a value on this sort of stone were in the Executive Office at 25th Street and Fourth Avenue. Finally, although the potential pledger could navigate, he was drunk as a skunk, and really not alert enough to supply information about his credentials, short of being nursed through a lengthy interrogation by someone who had the privacy and the time to conduct it. So off he was sent in a taxi to discuss matters with Munroe Bates.

When he arrived, Munroe saw immediately that nothing very lucid was likely to emerge from him, and asked if he knew someone else responsible who could talk for him and vouch for his ownership. The gentlemen was quite aware that he was cockeyed to the gills, and didn't resent Bates's suggestion at all. It even seemed to amuse him, and he tossed a pocket address book on the desk, mumbled out a name, and asked Munroe if he could call that number and explain the situation. The name was instantly recognizable, one of the most prestigious lawyers in New York, and when Munroe reached him on the telephone and mentioned the prospective borrower's name, he said he'd be right over. He arrived, established the man's identity (which didn't mean a thing to any of us—no one present had ever heard of him), and gave his own guarantee that the cuff links belonged to our inebriated guest. He was an actor, we were told, out of work for a long time but with a chance to land a good role, and he needed the loan to go off to a clinic, sober up, and have his tryout. The loan was made.

Months later the play *Harvey* opened on Broadway and became an instant, long-running hit. For those who never saw it, or the equally successful movie made from it later, starring James Stewart, Harvey was an invisible six-foot rabbit that no one other than the alcoholically-inclined hero was able to see, much less talk to. In the original stage version the hero was Frank Fay, and Frank Fay had been our friend with the star-sapphire cuff links. Clearly he had used the loan well, had landed the job, and was now creating one of the more memorable comedy roles of our time. We who had seen the inebriated Mr. Fay previously, under closer range than across the footlights, appreciated how wonderfully convincing and charming he was, acting a drunkard's role while cold sober. At least we presume he must have been sober, for Harvey ran on Broadway a very long time with Fay doing a superb job each weekday evening and on two matinees, and a man's liver can only take so much.

Another time a man walked into the Times Square office with some outstandingly attractive jewelry, obviously worth the loan he was seeking and more, but Sol Glicksman had to tell him he was sorry, but that he would have to go to the Executive Office.

It turned out, as Munroe Bates relates it years later, that the man was a very prominent lawyer from the Midwest who happened to own, among other things, a three-year-old racehorse, bred from an exceptionally good thoroughbred strain. Entered for the Kentucky Derby almost from the moment of birth, which is what an owner has to do if he has a horse he eventually hopes will be good enough to compete in the "Run for the Roses," the moment was now at hand for the lawyer to post the final entry fee. Apart from that, he wanted to place a large bet on his horse to win, but it wasn't convenient to lay his hands on ready cash just then. He had all the personal identification anyone might require, and his wife's affidavit stating the circumstances and giving her consent to the pledge. Munroe Bates quickly arranged for the transaction to go through the branch office downstairs, and a few minutes later a messenger arrived back in Munroe's private office bringing the requested $5,000 and the loan ticket to the lawyer. Meanwhile, he and Munroe had become bosom pals, exchanging medical histories because the lawyer had an intestinal complaint and didn't know any doctors in this strange city. Bates furnished him with a recommendation to his own physician, and in return the lawyer offered to get a bet down for Munroe on his horse in the Derby. Munroe had to refuse as graciously as possible, which was just as well. The lawyer's horse finished out of the money. On the other hand, two weeks later he won the Preakness!

In a completely different vein, one other sports story connected with the Provident comes back to mind. Toward the end of my years there I was in charge of the auction sales, and at least in cursory fashion examined every one of the articles going up for sale each month.

Doing this one day, I came across a modest item that struck a real personal chord. It was listed to be sold with all the unredeemed silver collateral, but like many such items was not solid sterling silver but plated. Plated articles in the Provident's sale fetched practically nothing, since they had no melt-up value at all. I made up my mind to buy the piece when it went on the block—if, as I felt sure would happen, it didn't cost more than about a dollar. Sure enough, when the time came I was able to secure it for just about that sum, and this was the one and only time that I ever bought anything at one of the sales for myself.

Well, I already was one fat dollar out of pocket, but for the sake of a gag I was ever a sport. I paid an engraver some fantastic price like another two or three dollars to do a job on my article. Then I managed to lay hands upon a Tiffany & Co. gift box of sufficient size, wrapped the piece carefully in tissue, and addressed it to Mel Alexander, the outstanding young golfer in our Long Island community years before, when we had been the closest of friends.

Obviously I was not present when he opened the package, but I could visualize his reaction when he undid the wrappings, took out the silver-plated trophy cup, and read on its front side the inscription:

Woodmere Country Club
1933 Mens Championship
Melville Alexander, Jr.

That was familiar enough. But when he turned the cup around he saw the new inscription on the back:

> Provident Loan Society
> 1938 Auction Sale
> Re-presented to
> Melville Alexander, Jr.
> from his friendly pawnbroker

CHAPTER 4

The Quiet Men

Archer. Boylan. Callahan. Casey. Cavanagh. Doyle. Farley. Finnegan. Flynn. Geraghty. Gallagher. Hogan. Kelly. McAuliffe. McMahon.

The names of the staff members of The Provident Loan Society, and particularly those who rose to the responsible jobs of becoming appraisers and managers of the branch offices, have read like a roster of the descendants of Tara and the other legendary kings of Ireland.

O'Connell. Quinlan. Quinn. Riley. Slattery. Tolan. Walsh. Yeats. It was hard to call out, "Hey, Pat (or Mike or Mary or Agnes, for that matter), have you an eraser?" without two heads turning and two hands being extended.

There are those critical of the Society's employment methods, particularly in the years about which I write, who place the blame for the preponderance of Irish Catholic staff upon the favoritism of the personnel manager of that day, and there probably is a large measure of truth in the claim. In any event, the situation is no longer so. And to do some justice to the old and long since passed away personnel manager, he was following a perhaps unknown history and tradition of the pawnbroking business.

From the earliest days, pawnbroking has been an Irish heritage from generation to generation, despite the modern impression that it has been chiefly Jewish. Even the two big and responsible private pawnshops during the 1930's were Irish, Simpson's and McAleenan's.

That is why, when James Speyer returned from Europe after his reconnaissance of the Mont de Piété and set out to find what then seemed to be the proverbial needle in the haystack, an honest pawnbroker, all replies centered upon one Irishman and one man only, a Bowery pawnbroker named Joseph Keane. Speyer invited Keane to visit him one day at his city mansion, and was extremely impressed with the man. Joe Keane was impressed too, reporting first the fabulous rooms and furnishings of the establishment at Madison Avenue and 38th Street and how awed he was by it all and by all the neighbors. You were likely to run into a nice class of person next door. J. P. Morgan lived almost across the street, for instance. Keane went on rapturously to report the offer Mr. Speyer extended to him:

"I was making $25 a week in the Bowery, and that was a mighty good living wage then. Mr. Speyer said that if I came to the Provident I would get a full five dollars a week more— $30 a week—and usually no one went up the salary ladder that fast in those days. So the extra money was wonderful enough, but the best part of it all would be that the hours would be so much better than what I'd been working. On this new job, there was to be no night work at all, and no Sunday work! Just a six-day week from a little before 9 o'clock in the morning until closing at 6 o'clock in the afternoon! It sounded like absolute Heaven!"

Joe Keane joined the Society to be its first appraiser on May 24, 1894, and stayed until ill health forced his resignation on August 11, 1927, always maintaining his reputation as the city's best, most considerate, and most honest of pawnbrokers. It may well have been his performance and reputation that influenced the hiring of so many Irish in later years. He was the model for the particularly warm and unique relationship that so frequently sprang up throughout the Provident's later history between certain of the Society's regular customers and the local branch office manager, who usually stayed many years at the same branch before being shifted to another. The Society effected such transfers now and then as a policy matter, and the rationale for doing so is an interesting one.

In the span of the three and one-half decades between Joe Keane's taking over the managerial reins of the first office, and the highly scientific methods of establishing fixed and consistent appraisals that were introduced in the early 1930's (described in detail in the next chapter), former commercial pawnbrokers like Keane were hired to run the ever-expanding number of offices of the Society. Commercial pawnbrokers have always had a hard time competing with the Provident Loan, because the Society has always offered lower interest rates, greater security, the potential for bigger surpluses if one's loan had to be sold at auction, and usually an altogether more pleasant atmosphere for conducting business. The one thing that a commercial establishment could do to attract pledgers away from the Provident was to offer larger loans, and they were very likely to do so. The Society's lending principle was that all men are created equal and that the same article justified the same loan regardless of who pledged it. What is more, that loan invariably was conservative, being set at a figure that the Society's appraiser figured was safe in case the article was not redeemed.

On the other hand, the commercial pawnbroker, his own boss and usually a one-man operation with no more than a clerk's assistance, was likely to take a chance on an old customer whose past record of regularly redeeming his property had been established. The pawnbroker, spurred by the profit motive that didn't exist with the Provident's appraisers, might go well past a reasonable limit and issue an excessive loan, feeling confident that it would be redeemed.

Men like Joe Keane and the other managers who had formerly been commercial pawnbrokers found it hard to shake this tradition in which they had been brought up, no matter how soberly the Society's Executive Office cautioned them about treating customers impartially. They would know from previous experience that one man was a regular big bettor on the horses, and that he invariably redeemed whatever he had pawned the moment he hit a few winners. They would know that a certain actress, temporarily out of a job, never failed to land work within a matter of weeks, and that she too consistently redeemed her jewelry once she was again drawing a salary. Why not lend people of this sort what they were asking, even if the sum appeared a little risky if a stranger were seeking it? The pawnbroker figured there really wasn't any risk, he would collect more interest, and he'd be doing a favor for someone he had almost come to regard as a friend.

Nor should you think that such cases were isolated and infrequent. David F. Cohen, for more than a quarter of a century the President of the Pawnbrokers Association of New York, is a lawyer with a practice on Fifth Avenue opposite the New York Public Library. He told me that "customers"—people who patronize commercial pawnshops again and again—have always been responsible for more than half of all the loans they make, and this holds true right up to the present day. It has always been the relationship that sprang up between that sort of borrower and the pawnbroker that has enabled commercial shops to go out on a limb in making loans that the Society wouldn't approve their appraisers making.

Such a relationship could neither be born nor flourish unless the same pawnbroker remained in the same shop over the years. During those earlier decades of the Provident's history, before a scientific and implacable lending schedule was devised, the managers, who were all commercial pawnshop alumni, quite understandably were likely to follow their old customs. Eventually the Executive Office started noticing that certain managers, who had been established in one office for a long period of time, were making an unusual number of bad loans. Investigation showed that this was not incompetence, but rather the result of misplaced confidence in borrowers who had become their favorites and who, after a consistent record of always redeeming their goods, suddenly did not. It was out of this experience that the Society inaugurated its policy of shifting a manager from one office to another after a period of time.

The policy did have its drawbacks from a public relations standpoint. Very often screams of protest arose from the faithful pledgers, who objected to the removal from their locality of someone they had turned to as Father confessor, psychiatrist, and even in one notable case, physician. In many instances someone would come into an office for a loan, brush off the strange face that appeared at the window, and demand that he deal, let us say, with Mr. McGowen.

"Mr. McGowen has been transferred from here (the Flatbush office) to our Fordham Road office. I'll be glad to take care of you."

Such a reply was likely to elicit an immediate freezing of the customer's attitude and tone of voice. Frowning and muttering about writing a letter to the Executive Office concerning this outrage, the person would demand instructions for reaching the Fordham Road office, which was approximately a thirty-mile round trip by subway or elevated train. He would then make a dignified exit and proceed to take off on the first leg of the trip. Arriving at Fordham Road about an hour later, a warm reunion with Mr. McGowen would take place.

"You *are* The Provident Loan Society for me, Mr. McGowen. What the devil are they thinking about to put you way up here? What can you lend me on this ring? The wife's much better, thank you, and how is yours? And while you're looking over the ring, let me ask your advice about . . ."

This intense loyalty to certain branch managers was shared both by men and women pledgers, and the impressions of those who have told me stories about it indicate that there probably were even more such cases among the latter than the former.

After telling about the predominance of the Irish, it is perhaps paradoxical to single out, as a prime example of an intense personal relationship, an office manager named Sol Glicksman. Sol was one of the comparatively few Jews in such a post, and he ran the Times Square office. Its location meant that it was likely to have the greatest variety of famous or at least notorious patrons, and probably the most loquacious. More occurrences of dramatic or human interest were likely to transpire in Times Square than, let us say, in the Hunts Point office in the Bronx. This meant that the Society needed a particularly astute and benevolent manager to handle the zany characters who were likely to patronize Times Square, and Sol had the same expertise, combined with wisdom and affability, of the best of his Irish confreres. He even boasted an extra attraction for some pledgers: Like Lucy in the Peanuts comic strip, he freely dispensed unauthorized and non-American Medical Association advice.

Many of the other old-time appraisers who knew certain pledgers well would listen to tales of woe or triumph, and would shake their heads sympathetically or offer congratulations as the case might be. Often their advice would be solicited about everything, from whether to go to the mountains or the seashore on vacation, or if Junior should be allowed to use the family car. But no one, except Sol Glicksman, was the fount of wisdom for so many pledgers plagued with headaches, hangovers, hemorrhoids, and fallen arches.

Sol had two drawers full of over-the-counter remedies. He had used all of these and believed in them thoroughly, and what Sol recommended was good enough for his customer friends, particularly when he never sent a bill. He practiced medicine—short of surgery—for decades without a license, and no one ever accused him of doing anything improper. There is no way of telling how many people got well because of, or despite, Sol's medical advice, but when he died the funeral was a standing-room-only affair.

Of course, not only the AMA but also the Provident's Executive Office authorities never knew about Sol's extracurricular activities, for with their exemplary ethical outlook they undoubtedly would have put an instant stop to it. The only ones who knew were the two or three other employees in his office, and the many pledgers who were being treated at this free dispensary. The employees worked under Sol and loved him, so they never squealed until after he was gone. And it probably would never have occurred to the pledgers that Sol was doing anything that wasn't exactly kosher.

Sol was a Provident manager first and foremost, however, and his medicine was merely a sideline. So one day, while he was attending to a customer seeking a loan at one window, another was presenting a ticket at a different one and pushing money across the counter. The ticket specified that the collateral was a diamond solitaire ring, which the man wished to redeem. He had the necessary cash to pay off the principal and the small amount of interest that had accumulated, and Provident Loan tickets are completely negotiable, so that unlike the requirement of proof of ownership at the time of making a loan, anyone holding a ticket can redeem an article. Provident tickets, if lost, should be reported immediately to the Society so it can place a "Stop" on the redemption process, but it's quite legitimate to sell one's ticket to a speculator who knows that the face value of the loan is almost certainly much less than the collateral is worth. All over New York there were establishments advertising in their windows, "Provident Loan Society tickets bought here."

So there was no reason for Sol to pay any attention to an apparently normal redemption that someone else was carrying out, particularly when he was busy himself. Nevertheless, after the vaultman had secured the package containing the ring, unwrapped and untagged it, and was about to hand it over, a strong set of fingers reached out and grasped his wrist, pulling it back before the ring could be placed in the outstretched palm of the man on the other side of the wicket.

"Where did you get that ticket?" inquired Mr. Glicksman.

"What business is that of yours?" was the retort. The man obviously knew that Provident tickets need not be held by the owner.

"Usually, none. But I know this ring and I know who owns it," said Glicksman, "and I want to be sure you have a right to it."

"Sure," said the man. "It's a woman's ring and it doesn't take a genius to know it isn't mine. But she gave me the ticket and the money to redeem it for her, and you haven't any right to interfere."

"Let me worry about my rights," said Sol. "I've seen that ring here too many times, and each time pledged by her and redeemed by her, not to look into this. The cashier will give you back your money, but I'm hanging onto the ticket and the ring until I can check this out. Meanwhile I'll give you a receipt for the ticket and will return it to you and apologize if she confirms your story. If she doesn't, you know what you can do with the receipt."

The man had no alternative but to accept his money back, pocket the receipt, and leave. It was still morning, shortly after 10 o'clock, and Sol telephoned the woman's number, waking her up. After identifying himself and saying he was sorry he had disturbed her, he asked her where she kept her ticket for the ring.

"In my bureau drawer, where I always keep it. Why?"

"Look and see if it's there."

Seconds later a shriek, so piercing that Sol had no difficulty hearing it even though the woman was nowhere near her end of the phone, was followed by a hysterical voice on the wire. Sol told her to calm down (and may have prescribed a sedative) and come over to the office. Fifteen minutes later, with clothes hastily thrown on, she appeared.

Sol was a trusted confidant, and it didn't take her very long, after he told his story, for her to confess that her hospitality to a stranger the previous evening had extended itself to asking him back to her room to share her bed. She had been surprised when the telephone rang not to see her guest present. Sol gave her an aspirin, returned her ticket with a lecture about storing it more safely in the future, and may well have added a few words of fatherly counsel about indiscriminate sex habits, although there is no evidence about that.

Life in the Times Square office went on as it had before, with Sol's next customer impatiently stamping one foot while rebuffing the perfectly capable services of another appraiser, maintaining that he was "waiting for Mr. Glicksman."

In connection with stolen goods, The Provident Loan Society and all other licensed pawnshops daily turn in to the Police Department a record of every loan they make. Each time the police can connect a reported theft with the description on a pawn ticket report, they place a "Stop" on the redemption of the article. If the true owner can establish his or her rights to satisfy the police, the pawnbroker must relinquish the collateral to the true owner. He has no way of being made whole again for the money he lent on it, unless the thief comes back again to try to redeem the goods, and that simply doesn't happen. If it did, it's problematical just what the pawnbroker might try to do about it. Pawnbrokers can be licensed to carry arms, but even if they do own a pistol, how often would one risk a shoot-out in such circumstances? The probability is that a thief, attempting to reclaim something he pawned illegitimately and meeting with any show of reluctance from the pawnbroker, would flee the shop before anything could be done.

Stolen goods that must be returned to the owner without any compensation to the pawnbroker constitute one of the hazards of the business. However, if you are thinking of going into it, there is some consolation in the statistic that reclaimed stolen merchandise only amounts to a tiny fraction of one percent of a pawnshop's business.

On some few occasions a Provident Loan representative finds himself drawn into someone's personal problems, and may solve them by means that aren't directly connected to the Society's business. There was a postman one time who, apart from carrying out the Post Office's boast that he would deliver the mail through rain or snow or heat or gloom of night, paid daily attention to the needs of an elderly man along his route. This man was so ill as to be housebound, so the postman invariably brought him a carton of coffee and a morning newspaper when he delivered the mail. Just before the old man died, he gave the letter carrier a ring with a large, rounded, blue-gray stone in it.

The postman wore the ring so that his donor could see it each morning, but when his old friend died he knew he could use some money better than he could the ring, for these were the Depression days and a letter carrier's salary had to be stretched to be able to stagger along through that rain, snow, heat, gloom of night, etcetera. He tried to pawn the ring at a pawnbroker's shop along his route, and as a result landed up in the local police station. For the pawnbroker had notified the police that a postman, who could identify himself but could not prove ownership at all, was attempting to pawn a ring that he suspected could not be his. His story sounded unbelievable.

The police apparently thought so too, for while they released the postman, they turned the ring over to the city's lost property office. The office kept the ring a year, and then, as the law requires returned it to the postman with an accompanying letter stating the facts in the case and establishing the fact that now the postman did indeed legally own the ring.

Still needing money, even more than before, the postman decided to try again. This time he had the good fortune to make his way to a Provident Loan office. Asked what he wanted in the way of a loan, he hesitated whether to inquire if he could get the $10 he felt he really needed. He didn't want to annoy the appraiser by asking for an unreasonable sum, and thought about settling for $5. But compromising quickly in his mind, he blurted out, "Seven?"

The appraiser, who had been studying the splendid star sapphire under his jeweler's loupe, replied that $700 would be quite all right.

When they revived the postman, perhaps with smelling salts, he explained that he was seeking only a $7 loan, which the Provident, never one to encourage a person to borrow more than he needed, was quite willing to make.

The postman pulled himself together. "You mean you'd be willing to *lend* me $700 on this ring without any question about it? Doesn't that mean that it's worth even more than that?"

The appraiser assured him that it did, but that The Provident Loan Society was purely in the lending business and did not purchase jewelry. However, if he wished, he would write a loan for him now for the maximum amount he felt he could offer—probably something in excess of the $700 he thought had been the request—and then the postman would have the option of redeeming it if and when he desired. Or at the end of a year he could let it go to sale, and he would receive any surplus that might be realized then.

"No," said the postman. "If I can, I want as much money now as I can get. I'm ill, I have heavy medical expenses, and who knows if I'll still be alive in another year."

The appraiser called over the manager and explained the situation. The manager thought about it for a minute, then asked the postman to sit down and wait while he made a few telephone calls. Returning with a slip of paper, he handed it to the postman and said: "Here are the addresses of three honest and reliable jewelry dealers who know star sapphires. I have phoned all three and explained to each that you have a lovely ring to sell and are looking to get the best fair price for it that you can. I've told each one that I've also given you two other names, so you can shop around with all three of them and see which will offer you the most, without any embarrassment. The cards are laid out on the table for everyone to see. Good luck, and don't take a cent less than $1,500."

The next day the postman came back, delirious with joy. One of the dealers had purchased the ring for $2,100.

Jewelry, particularly diamond jewelry along with a great number of gold items of lesser value, constitutes most of the Society's collateral on which loans are made. Yet the charter allows loans to be made upon any article that justifies a loan under the conditions set forth in it. Thus it didn't confound the appraiser in a certain branch office when a man came in with a rather long, leather-bound, slim case, opened it, and took out a piccolo. There was no reason to refuse to make a loan on a piccolo, if the appraiser had any idea in the world what it was worth. His problem was simple. He didn't have the foggiest notion.

He telephoned the prestigious music store, Schirmer's, and inquired if he could safely lend the man the sum he was requesting, which was something less than $100. The Schirmer representative was accommodatingly polite, but he did have a lot of questions to ask, apart from the make of the instrument. Was the silver part marked "Sterling?" Was the mouthpiece gold, and if so, what was the karat indication? And so forth.

Every question was answered in a fashion highly satisfactory to the Schirmer expert, who then said the piccolo was easily worth the requested amount if the final and most important question could elicit an equally gratifying response.

"Does it work? Can it be played?"

The appraiser looked at the man, then at the instrument. He held up the phone.

"Can you convince my friend at Schirmer's that your piccolo is in working order? Just a couple of notes, if you will."

A couple of notes indeed! The musician, out of a job and delighted to perform for this unexpected audience, struck a pose, launched into the *William Tell Overture,* and played it right through *fortissimo* to its final measure. Perhaps nothing so out of keeping with The Provident Loan Society's stolid dignity had ever occurred before, and probably not since. But the employees, the other customers, and the Schirmer man on the end of the telephone wire all burst into applause after he sounded his final sweet note.

He got his loan.

CHAPTER 5

How to Become a Diamond Expert

In the early days of the Provident Loan's existence, experienced pawnbrokers or jewelry dealers were lured away from their businesses by Mr. Speyer, or some other trustee, making an offer they could not refuse—such as Joe Keane's $30 a week. As the Society's business expanded, this type of trained, responsible person became impossible to find in the numbers that were required. By the time I joined the organization, the Provident had twenty-two offices entailing a group of about fifty appraisers. Where did they all come from?

Almost without exception they rose from the ranks. The use of a military term in this connection is appropriate, for the path of promotion was quite comparable. Competence, devotion to the job, and length of service were the factors that eventually pushed a young cashier into the better job of blossoming into a young-middle-aged vaultman, and finally into becoming the really esteemed middle-aged-to-old appraiser. The cream of this last group were also made office managers. Just about all of the office staffs had no ambition beyond that. As a group they were much like so many sensible enlisted men in the Army, and had no desire to take on the dull duties and responsibilities of a position in the Executive Office. After all, they were where the real action was.

So if the Kellys and Glicksmans were such outstandingly fine appraisers, how in the world did they get to be that way? Starting as cashiers, they handled nothing but money and loan tickets. As vaultmen they had the responsibility of working the combinations to the great doors, and wrapping, storing, and reclaiming collateral. But nothing in that job entailed jewelry knowledge or expertise. What good fairy descended from heaven and suddenly touched them with a wand to make them appraisers? Surely diamond experts grow out of years of dealing with diamonds, and learning to know them and their values. In the main it has been a family heritage, passed down to descendants in the Bowery, or West 47th Street, or Fifth Avenue, from grandfathers and fathers who were diamond merchants in Amsterdam or Antwerp. How did the Kellys and Glicksmans, with no such background, get into the act?

The answer has always been the envy and the mystification of the members of the professional diamond trade. They were envious because, whenever they needed a young appraiser in the business, they had to wait for the next boat from Amsterdam to see if one was aboard. They were understandably mystified, because the Provident's methods and terminology were completely different from anything they had ever seen or heard before, and yet the Provident people assuredly knew what they were doing! They seemed to know, for example, what a diamond would bring at one of their auction sales with considerably more accuracy than any but the most astute dealer did.

This apparent phenomenon has a remarkable explanation. Forced in its busiest days to produce something like fifty appraisers, when fifty appraisers simply did not exist to be hired, The Provident Loan Society solved the problem in its own, original, methodical, brilliant way. It devised a system and a training plan in which it could, in a relatively short period of time, create its own diamond appraisers out of nothing but willing and deserving applicants with good eyesight! Their grandfathers did not have to come from Amsterdam. They did not need to know anything about a diamond from the mineralogical standpoint. All they had to do was be taught four mechanical operations requiring good vision. Then they could find out what the Society would lend on such a diamond by using a book of tables, looking something like logarithm tables, which they had handy to their elbows.

In my early years with the Provident, I spent most of my time working on this project that ultimately caused such mystification to the professional diamond merchants. I'd like to take credit for devising it, but that recognition must go to the man whose engineering training not only conceived the grand design but worked out the details of how to execute it, Munroe Bates. Where I came in handy was that, as Munroe's assistant, I could perform a large part of the mechanical work for and with him, and I found it as fascinating as he clearly did.

Four factors determine a diamond's desirability and value:

1. size (expressed in carats)
2. color
3. freedom from internal flaws
4. excellence of the way it has been cut

Size is a simple matter of weighing, or of obtaining a close approximation of weight by the use of a caliper gauge. The Provident carries out this aspect of appraisal exactly the same way as do diamond men all over the world. But the men born to the business, and those who spend years in their trade, handle the other three aspects by virtue of their professional experience, knowledge, and "feel," or instinct. A Provident appraiser is taught merely how to look keenly, note, and then find the answer in a book. In the parlance of sport, there are "born" athletes and "made" athletes, and the Society's appraisers are "made." When they achieve proficiency, they can carry out everything about the appraisal function that the Society needs, but if they left to take a job with a jeweler, their background would be of surprisingly little help. Of course they would be equipped much better than someone who had never dealt with jewels before, but not as much as you might think, for they have been playing in another sort of ball game. Let's examine the four factors that have to be evaluated in a diamond, and see what Munroe Bates dreamed up to brew Instant Appraisers for the Society, as opposed to the traditional percolated brand.

Size. As indicated earlier, this is determined by the same methods, regardless of who is doing the determining. An unmounted diamond can just be weighed on a scale, and its weight is expressed in carats (spelled with a *c*, as opposed to the gold *k*arat), one carat being about 3 grains of troy or avoirdupois weight. However, most diamonds have to have their size determined when already mounted in a piece of jewelry, and of course this is always the case on Provident loans. No sweat. The proportions of a brilliant cut solitaire diamond (and almost all diamonds are brilliant cut) are consistent enough that, using a special caliper gauge to obtain its maximum width and depth reading, a very close approximate size of the diamond can then be looked up on a chart. It's the same principle as obtaining the area of a figure from its dimensions. A 1-carat stone, as viewed from above, has a width perhaps the size of a pencil eraser; a 2-carat diamond has a width more nearly that of a fairly large green pea; a 5-carat gem's width approaches the diameter of a dime; and the width of a 10-carat stone would be slightly larger than a nickel. The sizes of diamonds that fall between exact carats are expressed and written just as currency is; for example, when you see a stone marked "1.25 cts." you are looking at a one-and-a-quarter-carat diamond; another marked "2.58 cts." is a little over two and a half carats.

The size of a diamond is probably the most vital of the four elements that determine its value, because a diamond's price does not increase arithmetically as its size grows—it increases geometrically. In other words, a 2-carat diamond identical in color, quality, and cut to 1-carat diamond is not worth only twice as much—it is worth more like three times as much. A 3-carat stone will bring perhaps six times as much as a comparable quality 1-carat stone, and a 5-carat gem fifteen times as much.

When you get to even larger diamonds the geometric acceleration of the value per carat can leap upwards, far past the formula type of computation, and soar into the stratosphere. I am not speaking of a stone weighing 10 carats, which is big and unusual enough that most of us will never see one over the course of a lifetime. There are a sufficient number of these that I could make an educated guess that such a diamond would be worth fifty to one hundred times as much as its little 1-carat brother. But when one encounters the sort of diamonds that Mrs. McLean owned, or which Richard Burton used to buy for Elizabeth Taylor instead of bringing her flowers, there simply is no way of judging comparative values. Such a diamond is so rare that it becomes a front-page news item, is bestowed a name with all the pomp that a prince of the realm would receive at the baptismal font, and when it is sold is likely to bring any price that the buyer can bear. And the sort of buyer who can even contemplate buying such a gem can bear any price at all.

Color. Although there are diamonds of extraordinary color that command a tremendous premium value over comparable fine white gemstones, they are freaks. They are so rare that they fall beyond any general realistic discussion of the diamond. The Hope diamond, for example, with its absolutely unique blue color, is one of these. I have seen extraordinarily beautiful canary-yellow diamonds that, because of their clean, clear, and most unusual color, have been rated more highly by the cognoscenti than if they were fine white, whereas usually a yellow tinge in a diamond lessens its value considerably. Diamonds like the fine Canary type are colloquially termed "fancy-colored," and deserve this sort of mention here, but no more than that. At the Provident we encountered one every now and then, but when we did, it fell so far out of our normal purview that, if the loan sought seemed excessive by our usual standards for the size and quality of such a stone, we turned to specialists for an outside opinion. So let's forget the "fancies" and turn back to how The Provident Loan Society taught its bright-eyed, inexperienced men to judge the color of a diamond.

In the first place, "absence of color" would be a better term to describe desirability. The finest diamonds have no color at all, and what lessens their value is when traces of a yellow-ish tinge creep in or, still more damaging, a considerable amount of muddy yellow descending even to a rather light brown.

Jewelers in the trade who have handled diamonds over the years have a nomenclature of their own for the various shades (or absence of them), using words like "Jager," "River," "Wesselton," "Crystal," and "Cape." These men just peer at a stone through their jewelry loupes and decide what to term a diamond. They have no fixed standard to go by other than their experience and instinct. A "Jager" is the finest blue-white and a "Cape" is yellowish, and there are poorer gradations than "Cape," where a diamond has a distinct yellow or brown tinge.

For some years the comparatively few appraisers required by The Provident Loan Society tried to do the same, but as the number of offices grew and the number of necessary ap-praisers mounted, Munroe Bates decided to try to investigate the reliability and uniformity of the appraisals. He selected ten diamonds of obviously varying quality and had six office managers appraise them independently, under good and identical conditions. They all worked separately in the same room at the same time, under an excellent north light sky-light, exchanging diamonds as each finished his appraisal of the stone. Their average appraisals, from the lowest to the highest evaluation, varied by over 100 percent on the entire batch of diamonds, and by as much as 600 percent on one particular stone.

What Bates had suspected was true. These men all worked until 5 o'clock in the afternoon when, at least in wintertime in New York, dusk has fallen and street lights have been turned on. They couldn't possibly make the same determinations that they would make in daylight, and their judgments could not have any consistency. Additionally, each was located in a different branch office in the city. Some might have quite adequate or good lighting conditions in the daytime, with a north light window and no background across the street that would be a handicap, such as a yellow brick building; others might suffer from very poor lighting conditions. When brought together in one uniform test situation like this, each was inclined to judge color on the basis of his own particular working memories.

Munroe Bates tackled this problem with all the efficiency that might be expected from a man holding a degree in engineering. He obtained somewhat reluctant permission from the head operating officer of the Society (Bates being merely the Vice President in charge of the Appraisal Department) to indulge in what seemed at first blush an outrageous expenditure for the Society's benefit: the purchase of a great many diamonds to be used as test stones in the branch offices. Each office was to have a test stick, like a very long metal toothpick, on which was affixed in descending order of color approximately a half dozen diamonds, each about 1 carat in size. They would range from the finest at the top, to a diamond of rather poor color at the bottom. With twenty-two offices to be accommodated, this meant buying a lot of diamonds. But Munroe pointed out that if the time ever came that the purchases seemed an unnecessary or impractical extravagance, the diamonds could undoubtedly be sold with little or no loss, and even at a profit, considering the fact that they were being bought at so low an ebb in the nation's economy.

It took quite a long time to accumulate twenty-two diamonds almost identical as far as color was concerned, in each
of six gradations of color, but it finally was accomplished. A
test stick was presented to the manager of each office, and a
system of nomenclature was established quite unlike the
traditional one. Reading from top to bottom, the diamonds
were designated as FW (Fine White), W (White), VSO (Very
Slightly Off), and so forth down to BW (Biwater, an accepted
term for a yellowish-brown stone of quite poor color).

Now it was possible for anyone who had any sensitivity at
all to diamond colors to hold a diamond, on which he wanted
to establish the color, alongside the stick and move it up and
down until he decided it was most like one or the other of
the diamonds mounted on the stick. If it stacked up to the W
test stone, he would designate it as a White stone. If it wasn't
quite that good, but better than the VSO, the conservative
policy dictated that he classify it Very Slightly Off. The de-
lineation was quite clear to all appraisers after a comparatively brief period—days or a very short number of weeks,
rather than the years a diamond professional feels is necessary—and for the Society's purposes, each appraiser had a
tool upon which he could rely.

Flaws. Just as the percentage of Fine White diamonds in
circulation is an extremely small one, so is the percentage of
stones that are absolutely flawless. Almost invariably a diamond man will be able to spot some interior flaw in a stone.
It may be the tiniest of spots, not even visible through a six-
power glass but discernible when a ten-power lens is used.
It may be an insignificant white "feather" that in no way di-
minishes the diamond's attractiveness but does diminish its
value. And it may go all the way to large black carbon spots

that even the naked eye has no trouble seeing. (A diamond is actually crystallized carbon, and is composed of this one element only. It would seem possible that a diamond could be produced artificially, but of the numerous attempts to do so, nothing has ever been accomplished successfully other than the manufacture of not much more than microscopic specimens, not nearly worth the cost of the process.)

Bates called in several of our very best appraisers and, using me as the recorder and control of how the operation was to be carried out, set them to work examining literally hundreds of diamonds for internal imperfections. Let us say Mr. Hogan noted a pinhead-size inclusion, or carbon spot, in one diamond, located on the underside portion of the stone near its outside edge. The facets on top virtually obscured this flaw, and it could only be discerned upon very close examination under a high-power glass. Meanwhile, Mr. Archer had unearthed a flaw of exactly the same size and type in another stone, but this time it was dead center near the top, large facet (the table), upon which one looks down directly. A person with keen eyesight might see it unaided by a jeweler's loupe, and this was clearly a more serious defect than in the first case.

We had run off a great batch of line drawings, half of which were merely circles about the size of a nickel. The other half were the cross-section of a diamond viewed from the side. Mr. Hogan would indicate the relative size and character of the flaw he had observed on each of the two types of drawings, positioning it in each case so that we could tell just where the flaw existed. Mr. Archer would do the same with his observation. I would keep things straight, key the drawings to the appropriate diamond, and maintain the flow of the many examinations in an orderly fashion, so that each appraiser's determination was checked by at least one other appraiser.

We all then sat down around a large conference table for many weeks, comparing notes and opinions about the relative insignificance or severity of the flaws noted. Finally we came up with another original and arbitrary, but readily comprehensible, system of terminology. Flawless diamonds were to be classified as 0; the slightest of imperfections, such as might warrant a 10 percent depreciation, were to be labeled as 1; a more noticeable flaw as 2; and so on down to a really severe imperfection that might halve the value of a stone or depreciate its value even more, which would be a 5.

Once these determinations had been made, Bates and I commissioned a commercial artist to work from the rough drawings, and our interpretations of them, and produce a large chart. Under each of the numbers, and from both the top and side view, this chart depicted just what sort of flaw merited the appropriate number assigned to it. A couple of copies of this chart were furnished to each branch office, and now the appraisers had still another working tool that no professional diamond dealer had ever come across in his life.

Cut. "Cut" can mean either of two things as far as diamonds are concerned. There are various types of cut, apart from the overwhelmingly popular and traditional "brilliant cut," with its round circumference and 58 facets. Other types include the rectangle (or "emerald cut") and the square cut; the long, pointed-ends oval called the marquise cut; the pear shape; and the triangle cuts, among others. These are worth mentioning because they do exist, but almost as much as in the case of the fancy-colored diamonds, their numbers are comparatively insignificant and need not be discussed in any depth. By and large, diamonds are brilliant cut.

The other meaning of the word "cut" is how well a brilliant solitaire has been fashioned by the lapidary. This is what constitutes the fourth factor that can make a diamond vary widely in value, apart from the three previous considerations of size, color, and flaws. A lapidary is a very skilled workman, and it would not be incompetence that caused him to cut a diamond less well than the established standards dictate. He must study what is given him in the rough to figure out what is best to sacrifice in straying from perfection in the cutting, in order to achieve the most valuable result. For example, he may have a large moderately flawed stone where the maximum value potentially exists if he can emphasize its flashy effect. He might accomplish this by cutting the table too large and the crown too low from the standpoint of ideal proportions, and this may more than compensate for something of a loss in size. True, the diamond will lose brilliance if he makes this decision, because the proportions and angles of the brilliant cut are planned to obtain the maximum refraction of light into, through, and back upward and out through the table. When the lapidary deviates from the best standards, the brilliance of the diamond must suffer. But if a substantially larger stone, or even a larger-appearing stone, can be cut as a result, it can well be a sound commercial exchange to sacrifice some of the brilliance for the flash effect. Similarly, he may choose not to close the culet to the almost microscopically small facet it should be, because if he did so, he would have to shave the sides of the pavilion and the diamond would lose a substantial portion of a carat in its weight. (See the diagram on page 107 for what is meant by "culet" and "pavilion.") Finally, since diamonds are indestructible, a great many are always around which were cut when the technique for obtaining the most out of a brilliant cut wasn't the same as it is today. It was the practice and even the fashion in Victorian times, for instance, to cut the crown higher and the table smaller than modern judgment thinks best. Sometimes it's worth recutting such old-fashioned diamonds, but more often they remain as originally cut, and this means that the stone must be penalized in buyers' eyes when offered on the market today.

Munroe Bates approached this phase of creating Instant Appraisers in much the same way as when he tackled the flaws factor, but for me personally it turned out to be a long way from an instant piece of research. I spent every working day for about a full year carrying out his Master Plan, which involved measuring the way diamonds are cut by using an infernal machine Munroe and an engineering friend devised. At my peak performance I could measure twenty-five diamonds an hour, but let's call it an average of twenty. I worked an eight-hour day with an hour for lunch; call it a thirty-five hour week, because I forget whether or not, by this time, the Provident had stopped being open on Saturday mornings, the way all offices were when I first arrived. Fifty working weeks in the year supplies the last figure necessary to work out the following multiplication: $20 \times 35 \times 50 = 35,000$. Could I possibly have measured 35,000 diamonds? Almost surely not. Undoubtedly I had other jobs to do over that year, but I know very well that the number of measured diamonds must have run into the low tens of thousands. As Mr. Dooley once wrote (in effect—I quote from memory): "There was sivvin Guggenheim brothers worth fifty million dollars, or else there was fifty million Guggenheim brothers worth sivvin dollars—anyhow, the figgers was incredible!"

So were mine. I sometimes still dream about it.

How did this infernal machine work? A drawing of it will help.

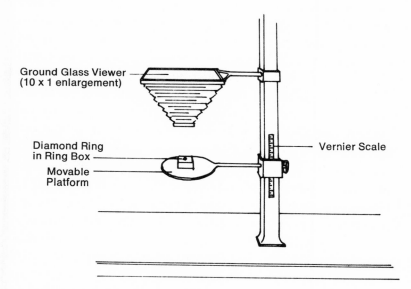

Essentially, the structure was just like the camera a photographer uses to take a picture of a small, stationary object. He looks down through a lightly-frosted glass mounted over a bellows, which he can adjust for focus and magnification. A strong light thrown at the object to be photographed, a moment of focusing, a clicking of the camera's shutter, and the photographer has done his work.

Would that my work had been so simple. But perhaps—would not. If it had, Munroe might have decided that 100,000 diamonds would be a nice round number.

The differences between Bates's contraption and the camera described was fundamentally twofold. Our gadget was not for taking photographs so it obviously had no lens. But the viewing, lighting, and focusing worked the same way a camera does. The photographer's camera was not for measuring diamonds, so it did not have what our device had built into it, an extremely accurate vernier gauge. This showed, in millimeters, exactly how much the platform that held the ring box in which the diamond ring was set was moving up or down. The examiner (me!) turned a small wheel to move the platform and thus make the critical vertical aspects of the diamond come into sharp focus. I would move the platform until the outline of the diamond's table sprang clear and sharp onto the viewing glass, then take a reading on the vernier gauge of just where the platform was at that stage. Next, I would wheel the platform up a bit until I had the girdle in sharp focus, and read the gauge again. The difference between the two readings would give me the height of the crown in millimeters. Continuing, when I raised the platform until the culet came into focus, and again read the guage, another subtraction would reveal the depth of the pavilion in millimeters. The sum of the height of the crown plus the depth of the pavilion gave the complete vertical depth of the stone.

We also had horizontal measurements to consider, but that was comparatively easy. The machine had been designed so that the image, when focused sharply onto the viewing glass on top, was exactly a ten-time magnification. All I had to do to obtain the three critical horizontal measurements—the widths of the table, girdle, and culet respectively—was to use a millimeter-scale ruler on them and divide my readings by ten. Since the magnification on the glass was tenfold, that division reduced the results back to the true millimeter measurement.

Using these measurements as data, we were able to work out what we felt were the ideal proportions for a brilliant-cut diamond, as well as the tolerable deviations on which no cutting penalty would be imposed in making a loan, for there are no absolute and exact rules for perfection. Tastes in cutting can vary a trifle without either of two slightly differing opinions being wrong, but they can't vary very much. When a crown is clearly too heavy or too shallow, or a culet definitely too open, a deduction has to be imposed, just as if the stone were flawed.

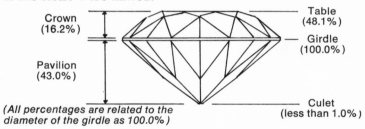

Crown
(16.2%)

Table
(48.1%)

Girdle
(100.0%)

Pavilion
(43.0%)

(All percentages are related to the diameter of the girdle as 100.0%)

Culet
(less than 1.0%)

Here is the profile of what we decided a perfectly proportioned brilliant-cut diamond should be. The table is just a bit less than half the diameter of the girdle, and the culet is as close to being closed as possible but short of coming to an actual point, for it is a real facet—one of the fifty-eight in a brilliant-cut—despite being so tiny. The depth of the stone should be approximately three-fifths of its width, with the ratio of the crown to the pavilion being about as shown.

However, as I had found out from bitter experience in studying all those thousands of diamonds, their cutting varies all over the lot away from an ideal standard. So now we had another detailed chart drawn professionally, much like the chart for flaws, and this one was also distributed among the office appraisers to show them what justified a penalty for its cutting, and what penalty to assess. Having used up the numbers 0 to 5 on flaws, we called cutting defects anything from 0, for a perfectly cut diamond, through 5, 10, 15, 20, 30, and 40 according to ascending severity of such defects. That chart appears below.

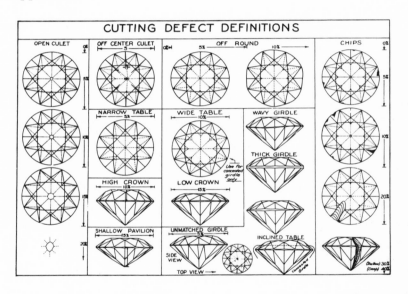

If a diamond contained more than one flaw, or had more than one cutting defect, the numbers were simply added together in each case. A combination of a 1 and a 2 flaw in one stone would be registered as 3: two 20 cutting definitions would invoke a 40 penalty. Sometimes this imposed a perhaps unduly severe judgment, but it was our traditionally conservative way of handling matters, and certainly was the simplest.

All of the foregoing meant that, in the end, a Provident Loan Society description of a diamond solitaire might read this way: 3.70 W 2-30. Translated, that would be a diamond almost three and three-quarters carats in size, of very fine but not absolutely top color, with a medium flaw that could be seen with a six-power loupe, and cut fairly poorly. Great stuff, but how did this help the poor inexperienced appraiser know how much to lend on that diamond? And wasn't that the point of all this hocus-pocus?

Up to this time, appraisers had been making all diamond loans on the basis of what a 1-carat stone was figured to be worth. They imposed arbitrary percentage deductions for stones that were off-color, flawed, or improperly cut. Apart from being wildly inconsistent, since the individual judgments of so many appraisers would obviously vary all over the lot, every element in this procedure tended to make loans absurdly conservative. Pinning loans on larger diamonds to the per-carat value of a 1-carat stone was in itself absurd because, as has been pointed out previously, the values mount geometrically rather than arithmetically as the size of a diamond increases. Instructing appraisers to make their own decisions about deductions for poor color, flaws, and cutting inevitably resulted in compounding such ultraconservative action. An appraiser knew that he wouldn't be criticized for a ridiculously low loan since, after all, the pledger may well have asked for no more than the sum lent. On the other hand, if his loan had mistakenly been too generous, and the article went to auction sale and resulted in a serious loss, eyebrows would be raised about that particular appraiser's competence.

The combination of glaring inconsistency and self-defeating conservatism in the making of loans is what set Munroe Bates's fertile mind thinking along the line described. Now that fertile mind moved to the next step, and once again moved my hands and body along with his mind into carrying out his plan.

We had frequently used the services of specialists at Columbia University for consultation, advice, and research into matters that required expertise outside of our everyday purview. A particular friend and associate at Columbia was Professor Paul Francis Kerr, who ran the University's gems and minerals course, which several of us attended at one time or another. Professor Kerr had worked with us on the early planning of the device to measure diamonds, but now that we were facing the problem of recording sales prices so that we could establish a proper loan schedule, we had moved out of his field of special knowledge. For this we probably needed a practical-minded statistician, and it just so happened that Kerr knew exactly such a fellow right up there at Columbia. An appointment was made to discuss the matter with him.

When we came into his office, we thought at first that he wasn't there. But as the door closed, a rather bald head emerged from out of a sea of papers, charts, and calculating machines to welcome us. Professor Blank—I regret that I don't recall his name, but that was the one and only time we ever met and he disposed of our problem in less than fifteen minutes—listened gravely as Munroe Bates told him what we had done so far, and what needed to be done next. I can only hope that you, good reader, have been able to follow my descriptions with anything like the immediate grasp that Professor Blank had of Munroe's explanation. It was deep calling to deep. After all, Munroe was an engineer, and engineers and statisticians basically have the same arrangement of little gray matter in their cerebellums. Professor Blank asked no questions at all, and must have pondered the complex question as long as ten seconds.

"What you need," he said, "are as many log/log graphs as you have categories of diamonds. The log/log feature should essentially give you a straight-line relationship, which you can read and project where necessary, if you plot the size of the diamond against the price it brings at sale. Now, if you'll excuse me, I'm quite busy."

Professor Kerr and I might as well have been listening to this dictum being delivered in Mandarin Chinese for all we could make of it. But Munroe Bates dug it at once, expressed our thanks, and we left Professor Blank forever. As I looked back for the last time, he was lovingly caressing one of the larger calculating machines.

On the way downtown, Munroe and I did a little calculating of our own. In our previous work we had established seven gradations of color, from Fine White down to Biwater; six gradations of flaws, from 0 to 5; and six gradations of cutting, from 0 to 50. Seven times six, times six, equals 252. That meant that under our system of classification of diamonds, there would be 252 separate categories, so we would need 252 sheets of log/log graph paper (whatever *that* might be) to carry out Professor Blank's brainwave. I went out and bought them in the biggest size obtainable, 22 inches by 22 inches.

Anyone familiar with a slide rule will not need an explanation, for the logarithmic principle is the foundation of that clever instrument. But for those readers who majored in the humanities, a log/log graph is one in which the intervals are not evenly spaced, as one is accustomed to see them on ordinary graph paper. Instead, the paper is marked off both horizontally and vertically in logarithmic intervals. When used, this shows a rate of change rather than the simple numerical change that ordinary graph paper depicts. A rate of change on a log/log graph depicts a constant geometric progression, such as the constant 100 percent rate of change when you double numbers: 1, 2, 4, 8, 16. . . . When Bates had indicated to Professor Blank that diamond prices mounted with increase in their sizes much more like a geometric rather than an arithmetic acceleration, the Professor had seen that a log/log chart would be the most likely tool to produce the sort of straight line that could best be utilized.

Over the following year, with big auction sales held every month, Bates and I plotted the results of well over 5,000 diamond solitaires. At the end of that time we had 252 well-filled charts, a typical example of which would be the one opposite for a White 1-10 stone (reconstructed today from memory of what such a diamond was fetching at a Provident sale in the late 1930's).

See all the little dots? Each represents a diamond whose description is W 1-10. The dot is placed above the weight of the stone (on the horizontal legend) and opposite the amount of money it brought at sale (on the vertical legend). For example, the dot indicating the diamond that was exactly 1 carat in size was sold for $200, whereas the dot representing the 2-carat diamond brought just over $600.

You can see that the dots do establish the pattern of a straight and remarkably narrow band. Our Columbia professor had known what he was talking about when he recommended the use of log/log charts.

With the occasional exception of a freak price that would fall higher or lower than such bands, this turned out to be true on all 252 charts. There is a complicated statistical tech-

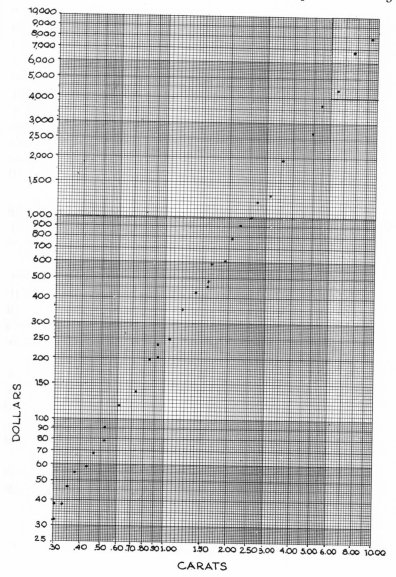

DOLLARS

CARATS

nique that can be used to fit the most accurate straight line into and through a band of this sort, but it can be done much more simply and with practically equal accuracy just by using a transparent ruler. If we now placed the top edge of such a ruler along the approximate center of the band, so that we could see how many dots fell above it and how many below it (we could see the latter because the ruler was transparent), we could jiggle the ruler's slant, and move it up and down, until we could see by inspection that the line we had established fitted the central pattern of the dots very closely. We drew the line and now knew, at least better than anyone else ever had been able to know before, what each size of W 1-10 diamond would sell for at the auction sale.

Still, this wasn't really the objective. What we were looking for was what amount should be *loaned* on each type of diamond, and of every size. It was smooth sailing to determine that, now that the research on sales prices had been done.

The Provident felt that it was appropriate to lend 75 percent of what an article would bring at auction sale. The difference would be enough to cover the interest and cost of sale, with a slight extra margin built in for conservatism's sake. So if we felt that a stone would sell for $200, the loan could be $150.

Now we had 252 lines on 252 charts that told us what diamonds had been bringing at sales in recent months. If we marked off points 25 percent below the ends of each line, and connected those with a new lower line parallel to the first, we'd know what the lending schedule could be, and you'll see this final version of the chart on the facing page.

Using this line and calling off the appropriate numbers one to another, Bates and I could then write out in tabular

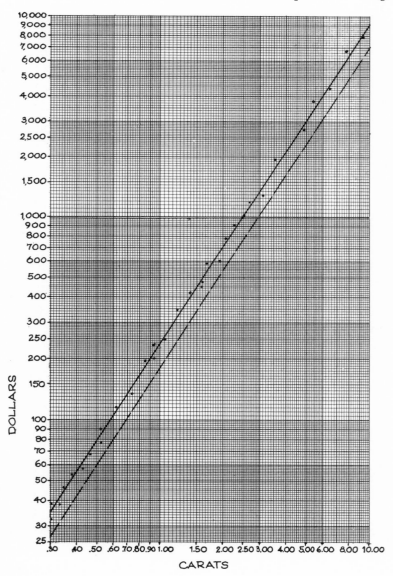

form a practical working tool for the office appraisers on each of the 252 classifications. In this case it would read partially as follows:

W 1-10

Weight	Loan
.30 carat (30 points)	$ 26
.35 ″	33
.40 ″	41
.45 ″	49
.50 ″	58
.60 ″	77
.70 ″	98
.80 ″	122
.90 ″	146
1.00 ″	170

And then, without showing the intermediate sizes here but merely picking off the loans on larger diamonds at half-carat intervals:

1.50 carats	$ 320
2.00 ″	510
2.50 ″	725
3.00 ″	975
3.50 ″	1250
4.00 ″	1550
4.50 ″	1875
5.00 ″	2200

Reading off the appropriate figures on the lower line in the same manner gave us the loan to be authorized on stones larger than 5 carats, all the way up to 10 carats, where the figure is $7,000. Any diamond that came our way that was bigger than 10 carats was a special case that had to be evaluated by extra considerations, but that happened infrequently.

We next prepared a book showing all the figures for every category of diamond, and had one printed for each appraiser. From then on, when one of them took in a stone, examined it using the techniques that Bates's black magic had wrought, and came up with the determination that he was looking at a W 1-10 diamond, or any other category for that matter, he did not have to ponder about what he should lend on it. He just took out his little book, ran his finger down the appropriate page until he found the weight (or size) of the diamond, and then read across in cold print that he should lend, let us say, $265 on this particular stone. Not $270 and not $260. $265.

Eureka!

This chapter has concentrated upon teaching you how to become a diamond expert, based upon my experiences from the 1930's. Would you like to read an interpolation about how to become a financial wizard, from the same source?

Part of appraisal technique for certain colored stones in those days involved the use of the then new product, Polaroid glass. It absorbs all the light except that vibrating in a certain direction, so glare can be filtered out to any extent desired by adjusting the axis of one sheet of Polaroid glass across the axis of another until the best nonglare effect is achieved.

We played around a lot with Polaroid in our gem laboratory, and for the one and only time in my life I was struck with the thought that, if I had any inclinations to plunge into the stock market (which I certainly did not at that time), and if I had any money to do so (which I even more emphatically certainly did not), I'd buy Polaroid stock. I presume you know what happened to Polaroid shares in the ensuing years, no matter what has happened to them recently. It was *the* glamour stock of the era, and anyone who had purchased it, even modestly, at the time of which I write would be living in a castle on the Riviera, and not having to write books.

That is how I almost became a financial wizard. It is unimportant to confess that the reason I thought Polaroid would be a good thing had absolutely nothing to do with the products, such as the camera, which the company put out later, and which were responsible for its gigantic success. No. I was convinced that every new automobile that was going to be manufactured would have its headlights made of Polaroid and set on a certain axis, while every windshield would also be Polaroid glass set at the appropriate axis to eliminate glare!

Forty years have passed, and I've never had another stock market hunch.

CHAPTER 6

All Is Not Diamonds That Glitters

Diamonds are a girl's best friend, as Carol Channing put it. She could well have added that they are also the borrowers' and the lenders' best friend as well, for a couple of reasons.

For one thing, despite the rigid controls that the South African diamond syndicates exercise to restrict annual world distribution, and so support the price levels, there are still a great number of diamonds in people's possession. The other precious stones, on which comparable loans might be made, are relatively scarce. Secondly, one diamond's size and quality can be related much more accurately to another's than can one of the other precious stones to its kin. That means that establishing a standard loan schedule, such as was described in the previous chapter, is not at all practical when an appraiser has to place a value on the other precious stones.

From the Provident Loan's standpoint, the "precious" stone is the only one that justifies any sort of sizable loan, and (this may surprise you) there are only four "precious" stones: the diamond, the emerald, the ruby, and the sapphire. The pearl is also considered "precious," but it of course is not a stone. All of the other lovely gems that you may see and very possibly prefer are "semiprecious" stones: amethyst, aquamarine, bloodstone, carnelian, cat's eye, fire opal, garnet, hyacinth, jade, kunzite, lapis lazuli, moss agate, nephrite, onyx, opal, peridot, quartz, rutile, spinel, topaz, tourmaline, turquoise, and zircon—to name a few of the more popular ones.

"Semiprecious" is an indeterminate and often misleading term, since it denigrates what may be a magnificent and costly cat's-eye or jade, while an ugly and almost worthless diamond or sapphire is still called a "precious" stone. The Provident Loan Society has always had to err on the side of conservatism in making loans, as has been explained, with the result that the simple and practical thing to do in my day was to disregard "semiprecious" stones completely—or almost completely—when extending a loan. Oh, certainly, if the neck-chain and precious metal mounting of a pendant justified a $24 loan by themselves, and the centerpiece was a handsome semiprecious stone, the appraiser might well take it upon himself to boost the offer to $30, but that was about it. This policy was not only unjust in many cases but also produced some remarkable and somewhat embarrassingly high surpluses at the auction sale. But on the whole it made sense. For one thing, the appraisers couldn't accumulate enough experience on such varied items to gain much solid knowledge of values when an article had particular and unusual appeal. Even more to the point, during the Depression semiprecious stones, with those few exceptions, were literally a dime a dozen. The jewelry dealers, disassembling an article for its breakup value, would toss semiprecious stones into a box, much as any of us will do with paper clips.

Today, with the antiques market so strong, semiprecious stones often command prices that make an old Provident Loan employee's eyes blink and his mouth water for the opportunities he missed years ago. Still, the conservative lending policy hasn't changed materially, because the Society can't average out good results against bad when articles are forfeited and go to auction sale. Each lot stands on its own, and if one fetches a price that realizes a handsome surplus, the pledger gets it; if another has a disappointing result and sustains a loss, the Society suffers it. The Provident can't win at the auction sales, which means that its ultraconservative lending policy really can't be faulted.

So, since this is a book about the Provident, semiprecious stones figure only in the occasional anecdote, inspired by some freak incident. On the other hand, the method used in appraising the "precious" stones, other than diamonds, was as fascinating as it was complex. It required such special knowledge that only three or four of us who had taken Professor Kerr's gem and mineralogy course at Columbia University were equipped to carry it out. All major nondiamond "precious" gems were referred to one or more of these trained people, all located at the Executive Office. The main assignment was in the hands of an older appraiser, George Constant, who dealt only with such stones in his later years with the Society. I was by far the youngest of the others who had learned about colored stones, and during the week each month when we described, evaluated, and catalogued the auction sale, I assisted George.

Sapphires, rubies, and emeralds are judged—like diamonds —by their size in carats, their color, flaws, and cut. These determinations require as much, or more, of an expert's eye as do diamonds. However, colored precious stones involve something else before any other considerations need be faced: Are they real or synthetic? It's often almost impossible to know without the use of scientific equipment. A diamond's unique brilliance is unmistakable to the trained eye, but a colored stone has to be tested. Mohs' scale of the relative hardness of minerals is the very first consideration when one is trying to determine whether a stone actually is what it may seem to be.

Mohs, whoever he may have been—the reference books don't seem to say other than he was a mineralogist named Friedrich Mohs—devised the following arbitrary scale: diamond 10; corundum 9; topaz 8; quartz 7; orthoclase feldspar 6; apatite 5; fluorite 4; calcite 3; gypsum 2; and talc 1. The divisions make no attempt to be equal, with the difference between 9 and 8 very much greater than any between the lower numbers, and the difference between 10 and 9 fantastically greater than that. The difference in hardness between the diamond (10) and the next hardest mineral, corundum (9), is greater than the difference between corundum (9) and talc (1)! No wonder that the diamond is regarded as something very special. Nothing in the world will come even close to scratching it, let alone cutting it, except another diamond. Things of greater hardness can scratch things of lesser hardness, which is why one should not throw jewelry together in a jewel box. Things of the same hardness can scratch each other. It's unlikely that one diamond would scratch another if laid carefully in a jewel box, but it would be sheer madness to toss in your opal ring (hardness of 5–6½) or your pearl necklace (hardness 2½–3) if the box also contains much harder jewels.

The sapphire and the ruby are both corundum, and they are the only gems whose hardness is 9. Yet that determination alone will not tell the appraiser that he is handling one or the other of these stones, for the synthetic sapphire or ruby will test equally well as far as hardness is concerned. The fact is that the synthetic sapphire or ruby also proves out exactly the same as the genuine in all other scientific tests except one—close examination under powerful magnification.

The basic tests for the colored precious stones consist of finding their specific gravities, or densities, and their refractive indices, or the measure of the amount a light ray is bent as it enters or leaves a substance. Both are expressed in numerals that can be ascertained by the use of delicate instruments, operated by trained experts. If you find, for example, that a stone has a hardness of 9, a specific gravity of 3.9–4.1, and a refractive index of 1.76–1.78, you know you are dealing with corundum and nothing else. *Unless* it's synthetic corundum. And to find out whether this is so or not, you have to examine it either with a strong jeweler's loupe or microscopically.

Genuine sapphires and rubies crystallize in nature, as do all gemstones, and in the case of corundum the crystallization is hexagonal. Thus as one peers into a sapphire or ruby, powerfully magnified, parallel and straight striation lines that form the color can be discerned meeting at a 60 degree angle. Also, one often can make out tiny crystal inclusions within the stone, and these, being hexagonal, have pointed edges. If you were looking at a synthetic stone, the striation lines would also be parallel but they would be curved, and what might look like crystal inclusions would be bubbles, and round. Don't ask me why synthetic gems producers, who are so clever at everything else, have never been able to lick these bugs, but they haven't.

Suppose you have run all your tests, conducted your microscopic inspection, and are ready to testify under oath in court that you have a genuine corundum jewel. But is it a sapphire or a ruby? If you are blue-red color blind, there would be absolutely no way in the world for you to say, unless some noncolor-blind trusted crony whispered the answer to you as you took the stand! The sapphire and the ruby are exactly the same gem mineralogically, and only their respective colors differentiate one from another.

Sapphires and rubies can be flawless, or close to it, but their major value usually reposes in how fine their color is. A magnificent fine blue sapphire, or deep red ruby, that contains a flaw will not be depreciated in value to anything like the same extent as will a comparable diamond. Even the cutting, which has to be good to retain the maximum refractive index quality of brilliance, is not judged too severely if the color is superb.

Some sapphires and rubies are cut cabochon, which means they are unfaceted and the top is shaped into a dome, smoothly polished. If cut in the correct crystallographic direction, such stones display a rayed figure by either reflected or transmitted light. And since corundum crystallizes hexagonally, that figure is a six-line asterisk. These are known as "star sapphires" or "star rubies," which can also be very valuable, although their colors are rarely anywhere near as deep as the gem sapphire or ruby. Star sapphires range from light blue through light purplish to gray; star rubies from pink to purplish and, in the latter case, it is hard to know if the stone is a star sapphire or a star ruby, even if one is not color-blind. Three of the most engaging memories I cherish from my years with the Provident have to do with a sapphire, then with rubies, and finally with emeralds.

The Sapphire Story

George Constant, an outstanding branch office manager for years, had turned a trifle cantankerous in his sixties and was less urbane and friendly to customers than he had been before arthritis started to trouble him. The Provident in its infinite wisdom recognized George's unusual aptitude as an appraiser, and knew he was the very best of the lot in judging colored precious stones. So the Society shifted him permanently out of contact with the public and set him up in his own private laboratory in the Executive Office, to handle colored stones exclusively and to be the authority on such loans. That was his sole assignment every working day, but once a month he was also to examine, describe, and put a starting price and anticipated sale price on each colored precious stone slated to be sold at auction that month.

Pricing was a big job, which usually took a full week to accomplish. If George was to carry on during those special weeks with his regular job of determining loans on colored stones collateral, he needed help. Since I was young, had done extremely well in Professor Kerr's gem course, and seemed a logical successor to George in the field, I was assigned to be his assistant during that one week a month preceding each auction sale. I left my own office at those times, bunked in with George in his laboratory, and each of us whiled away the golden hours bending over our respective spectroscopes and refractometers.

At that time the Provident divided its monthly sales between the fashionable uptown auction gallery of James P. Silo and the unfashionable Bowery auction rooms of Jacob Shongut. Attractive and expensive items were booked into the Silo sales; items that would be sold chiefly for breakup value went off to Shongut's. Although we shared opinions now and then, on the whole George was responsible for handling what was scheduled for Silo's, and I for what was going to Shongut's.

One day I picked up an article destined for the Shongut Bowery sale, which consisted of what was obviously an immense, deep blue, pear-shaped hunk of glass, strung as a pendant on a very thin gold chain. The Provident local office had made a loan of $2 on the chain because, if the item ever went to sale, the assay price of the gold was approximately $3. The value of the blue glass was, in the Provident's eyes, no more than if it had been an empty milk of magnesia bottle.

Still, I ran the stone through the appropriate tests simply out of the conscientiousness that the Provident had instilled into me by this time. After I had subjected it to the entire process I handed it over to George, who normally was above being bothered by Shongut items, and said, "What do you think of this?"

George went through the same catechi. as I had just completed, scratched his head, and said, "I see what you mean. It's ridiculous, but it seems to be a genuine Burma sapphire of exceptional color, weighing just over 130 carats!"

Both George and I tended to believe our eyes, but the entire situation was too much for our reason. It was so illogical that this pendant, worthy of being a museum's most prized piece, should be going to auction sale for $2 and small change to redeem it, that we didn't want to go out on a limb without outside, authoritative confirmation.

The Provident always has been on very good terms with the most prestigious of Fifth Avenue and Park Avenue jewelers, including Tiffany's, so Munroe Bates and I made an appointment with the greatest authority on sapphires we knew. That afternoon we trotted uptown with our curiosity in my pocket. The Great Man did just what George Constant and I had done, plus a couple of other particularly recondite operations that our Columbia gem course had not thought worth bothering us about, and came up with the same conclusion: a genuine and extremely fine Burma sapphire, weighing 132.46 carats.

Well, to place the pendant on sale at Shongut's would clearly be an act of madness, but it didn't strike us as being very sensible to shift it to the Silo sale either. The regular professional jewelers' clientele at Silo's were essentially diamond men. A private individual might conceivably bid on a magnificent, expensive sapphire, but would we be likely to get even one such person at the sale, to say nothing of more than one? No. The stage clearly was not likely to be set for a wildly contested series of bids.

To gain time, we withdrew the pendant from the sale for that month, got in touch with the pledger, and asked her to come to the Executive Office and see us "on a matter that may be to your interest." She soon arrived, a middle-aged lady of clearly modest dress and circumstances, accompanied by a constantly screaming young child whose chief complaint was that she hadn't had lunch and wanted to be anywhere else than at 346 Fourth Avenue. It was hard to hear the mother's answers as Munroe Bates asked her how she had come into possession of the article she had pledged.

"It was a twenty-fifth-year anniversary present from my father-in-law."

"Who was he, and what did he do?"

"He was a big building contractor. He's dead. So is my husband."

"Well, did he tell you what it was, and did he give you any idea of its value?"

"No, but he said it was worth a lot of money."

"In that case, why did you pledge it for two dollars and then disregard it, despite our notices to you that if you didn't do something it would go to public auction?"

"Well, I needed the two dollars, and that was all the man would give when I brought it in. Now today I still need the two dollars, and whatever more it would cost to get it out. Anyhow, I've no real use for it and I don't even like it that much. Besides, I knew that if the Provident got more than two dollars for it at your sale, you'd turn it over to me. That happened to me once before on a watch I had, and I got almost ten dollars more than I'd borrowed!"

We investigated the woman's story, and it stood up. Her father-in-law had indeed been quite an operator, with connections ranging from politics to the Mafia. He had frequently been in the chips sufficiently to have been able to purchase such a costly item as this one. We had no police report on the article, and there was no reason to be suspicious of ownership any longer.

So we suggested that the woman redeem the pendant. If she didn't have the two dollars-plus we would lend it to her without further interest. Then we would see if we couldn't have it sold for her benefit through outside channels. She agreed, albeit a little wistfully because she had hoped to get a surplus of some sort this very month from our auction sale result. But we said we didn't think it would take too long. The fact is that one of the most glamorous Fifth Avenue establishments took the pendant on consignment the next day, and sold it within two weeks for something over $50,000. After deducting their commission, and after The Provident Loan Society had repaid itself the two dollars, our lady friend was able to take the Long Island Railroad back to her home in the Rockaways with a very, very fat check, particularly for Depression days. We all hoped that she spent at least a bit of it on a pacifier for her child, but if she did we never learned about it, for she was not seen again.

The Ruby Story

The telephone rang. It was one of our Irish Catholic appraisers, then stationed in the Pennsylvania Station office, and he was so upset that his words could scarcely be distinguished.

"Sure and there's an Indian fellow here with the most disgustin' thing I ever laid eyes on, and if it wasn't my duty to be polite and to make loans, I'd throw him out onto 33rd Street! But the thing is made out of solid 22-carat gold, and has a lot of little red stones that look like real rubies. I didn't want to soil my hands with the nasty object, but I went as far as testing the gold, since that's my job. But the rubies—if they are rubies—isn't my job, thank the good Lord, so *you* take this on, and I hope you not only don't give this blackguard a loan but maybe you can have him thrown in jail on a morals charge! Good day to you!"

I must say that Munroe Bates and I awaited the appearance of the "Indian fellow" with some anticipation. When he appeared, our expectations were more than exceeded. He wore a turban, spoke with an Oxford accent, and carried a large, heavy, wooden box such as usually houses a microscope. But when the wooden box was opened, it revealed another box of almost the same size, gleaming with the pure vivid color of 22-karat yellow gold and studded generously with red, ruby-appearing stones.

That was enough in itself to knock one's eyes out, but the real punch, which is what had upset our appraiser so thoroughly, was the series of small sculptured figures that had been fabricated onto the box as part of the gold. Male and female figures, all in the nude, each pair about to approach each other in coital positions that would make the artist for *The Joy of Sex* blush for his innocence. That is, the couples were approaching each other when the sliding top of the box was in its open phase. When the top was slid back, so that the box was closed, I need not describe what happened with respect to the new situations in which the various nude couples found themselves!

Munroe and I maintained discreet poker faces, and I put the box on the scales. Even without the added value of the rubies, the box was so heavy that the gold value alone came fairly near justifying the very sizable four-figure loan the Indian was seeking. When the rubies tested out as genuine, we didn't even bother to try to total up their maximum value. Instead we authorized that the loan be negotiated, the Indian accepted his money, made a gracious bow of thanks, and took his departure. I wondered at the time what sort of sensation that article would have produced had it ever gone to auction sale and been exhibited publicly, but that never happened. The box remained circumspectly wrapped in the Fourth Avenue office vaults until the day it was redeemed by its owner. But what an Oscar it would have made for *Playboy's* Best Fiction of the Century.

The emerald is cut from the mineral beryl, and is less tough and hard than the other varieties of beryl, whose basic hardness is 8. The aquamarine, a lovely "semi-precious" stone, is 8-hardness beryl, but the infinitely more valuable emerald is only 7½, and that's enough of a difference that emeralds have to be handled and stored more carefully than the other precious stones. Once again, the depth and luster of green in a splendid emerald is what counts most, for emeralds are almost always flawed, sometimes very severely, and one doesn't expect to encounter a specimen really free of flaws except on very rare occasions. Like the sapphire and the ruby, when a fantastically marvelous emerald comes onto the market it commands an even higher price than a diamond of similar size and quality. But when the colored precious stones are anything less than marvelous, they are not worth as much as their diamond peers.

An Emerald Story

Once upon a time—the time of which I write—a very aristocratic lady owned a pair of earrings that were really out of this world. They were so much out of this world that they never seemed to be in her world either, because through the years she constantly had a large loan on them, and they reposed in the vaults of one of the Provident's Upper East Side offices.

I was aware of this because, over the years that I was in charge of the auction sales at J. P. Silo's for the Society, annually these absolutely stunning earrings would be scheduled to be sold. And then the loan would be renewed by payment of the interest due, and the earrings would be withdrawn from the sale. The following year the same thing would take place. And so on.

No one who knew anything about jewelry could ever have seen these earrings and not remembered them. Each consisted of a magnificent square-cut emerald, approximately 20 carats in size, set in platinum and framed by small, fine white diamonds. I'm not sure I ever encountered another emerald as fine in all respects as each of these were: The color was the best emerald color imaginable and, almost unknown in emeralds of that size, there were no flaws at all that were visible to the naked eye. It was an aesthetic pleasure to be able to see them each year as George Constant and I were booking the goods scheduled to go to auction, although we were sure from experience that the owner would renew her loan and not permit the earrings to go on the block.

But there came a day, perhaps four years after the first time we ever saw the earrings, while we were booking the forthcoming sale, that we were brought up short in amazement. *One* earring—clearly one of that fabulous pair—but only one was among the collateral spread before us. How was this possible? Was it conceivable that the Provident had lost one, or that one had been stolen? Knowing the background, I felt I had to call the situation to Munroe Bates's attention to see if he thought we should investigate, even though we had no real reason to think anything was wrong.

Munroe listened and agreed that we should do something. The first thing, of course, was to check with the Upper East Side office and make sure that the loan in question consisted solely of one earring as collateral. It did. The next, as in so many other episodes, was to get in touch with the pledger, not for any benefit to the Society but for her own protection. In this case, we found out everything we needed to know over the telephone.

"How does it happen, Mrs. X, that your earrings are separated and you have a loan on only one of them? And do you realize that the auction sale is only three days off and, if you don't renew or redeem, the earring will be sold?"

"Yes, I know. This is what took place. Last year I had enough money to redeem the earrings for the first time in years, rather than renew the loan, so I did. Unfortunately, soon afterwards I did need money again, but not as much as usual, so I only pledged one earring. Things didn't get any better, so a few months later I pledged the other one, too. And now I'm going to have to let both go and hope I get a couple of big surplus payments."

"I'm sorry to hear that, but don't you realize that if the earrings are sold separately, they can't possibly realize anything like the price they would command if sold together? You have a really unique pair of emeralds here. None of us has ever seen two such gems, so perfectly matched in every respect. If one were to try to find still another that would match these in size, color, and freedom from flaws, it probably would take years, and it might well be completely impossible. Individually each will undoubtedly bring an excellent price, for each is a superb stone that can be made into something else, like a ring. But as a set, there's hardly ever been anything like them. It would be a crime to separate them, and we're certain that you'd be losing the very considerable premium that buyers would be willing to pay to acquire the two together."

"I hadn't realized that, but what can I do? I haven't the money right now to renew my loans, let alone redeem them."

We suggested that she allow us to take the one earring out of the current sale and hold it until the other one was due to be sold, some three months later. We would not charge futher interest on the first earring during those three months. At the end of that time, if she was in a position to renew or redeem, well and good. If she wasn't, at least we'd be able to sell the two earrings as one lot, and so obtain for her the best price possible. She agreed.

Three months passed and the owner's financial situation had not improved, so the emeralds did go to sale. They were a sensation at the first day's exhibition, and the word got around. On the day of the actual sale, we estimated that we had an extra two dozen dealers, and a couple of private individuals, who were attending solely to bid on that one lot.

The great moment came. The auctioneer announced: "Lot number 427, a pair of magnificent emerald and diamond earrings for which you have all been waiting. What am I bid?" A dozen voices, and signals from the floor, fought for attention at the starting price, and the bidding went up by leaps and bounds, first in $2,500 jumps and then in $1,000 overbids, well past what the Society would have anticipated had each earring been sold separately. At this point only two bidders were left, competing against each other in $500 increments, and finally one dropped out. The auctioneer raised his hammer, made a last plea for further bids, and began his chant, "Going . . . going. . . ." Suddenly a completely new voice—a feminine one—called out a new bid for an additional $500.

The dealer who had made the previous bid, and who must have thought he was about to secure the earrings, looked around in frustration and annoyance to try to see who this new bidder was. But sitting at floor level in the midst of a big crowd, he was unable to identify her. After a moment's pause he merely raised his catalogue again to indicate his willingness to go another $500. But I, seated next to the auctioneer on a raised platform, had been able to spot the bidder, and I was temporarily frozen to my chair in astonishment and indecision about what to do. It was Mrs. X herself!

I started to get down from the stand intending to work my way toward the back of the room where Mrs. X was standing. But before I could get very far, she had bid another $500. As I reached the halfway mark the auctioneer, completely unconscious of what had made me depart—and probably figuring that I had chosen a peculiar moment to visit the men's room—received and acknowledged the next $500 topping bid from the dealer. Bedlam burst loose in the room as Mrs. X, who had been standing next to the window grasping the long curtain that flanked it, fainted dead away, bringing down the entire curtain structure with her!

I fought my way through the crowd, reached her unconscious form, and told the Silo attendants that I knew her and please to help me carry her to Mrs. Silo's private office. We did that and, as the door was closed, I heard the auctioneer's chant finally reaching the last word as he knocked the lot down to the dealer: "Going . . . going . . . GONE!"

Mrs. X was pretty far gone as well. We revived her, and she sobbed out her explanation.

"I came just to see what price the earrings would bring. When it seemed that they were about to be sold, I couldn't bear it and decided that no matter what the cost, I had to get them back. So I bid."

"If you hadn't fainted, would you have kept going? Were you really just trying to run up the price, with no chance of being able to pay if you had been the successful bidder? In that case, and even without it, we owe it to your competitor to explain the situation and make some adjustment."

"I don't know . . . I simply don't know. I saw the hammer go up and I suddenly couldn't bear the thought of losing my emeralds. I hadn't come to the sale with any such intention, but something instinctive just made me try to save them at that point. It's crazy, but I still feel that way. I don't know how far I might have gone if I hadn't fainted. I don't know what to do now!"

I explained to her that there was nothing she could do now, except try to accept the situation. The dealer had purchased the earrings legitimately and they were now his. In fact, if anyone had something to do, it was The Provident Loan Society. The dealer had been forced to bid $2,000 more than was necessary to secure the lot, as the result of her two bids which we, knowing the whole story, had to regard as spurious. I would have to explain the situation to him and have the knock-down price lowered to the last bid he had made before she entered the picture. The Society couldn't countenance any lesser action, if its reputation for conducting completely honest auctions was to stand up. But if it was any consolation, I added, doing some quick mathematics in my head, she would be receiving one of the largest surplus payments in the Provident's history—possibly the largest—and that should go a long way toward relieving her financial pressure. Additionally, if she still was intent upon reacquiring her emeralds, I would tell the dealer that he had a possible customer in her, and I would give her the dealer's name and address so they might get together if she decided that, with her surplus money, she might be able to swing a repurchase. Wholesale jewelry dealers are usually content with a small percentage profit if they can turn over their risk purchases quickly, and she might well not have to pay much more than had she been the successful bidder.

Still weeping, but now quietly, Mrs. X thanked me, took the name of the dealer, and walked out of our lives, except for our Surplus Accounts Department's mailing of her check a few days later. I spoke to the dealer along the lines I had indicated, he took down her name and address, and I'm afraid that is the perhaps unfinished end of the story. Had the dealer been a regular New York patron of the sales, I could have found out whether or not Mrs. X reclaimed her emeralds. But he was not. He had made the trip from another city specifically because he was interested in this one lot, and to the best of my knowledge, he never returned again. That may well have been because the auction sale of so spectacular a matched pair of emeralds was a once-in-a-lifetime thing.

Pearls constitute the other form of jewelry considered "precious," although they obviously are not precious "stones." A true, fine pearl is composed of nacreous layers built up by a mollusk around a small central point, or nucleus. This nucleus must be unattached to its shell or the chances are that the pearl will not be round. The nacre is the attempt of the mollusk to kill and rid itself of the irritant nucleus, which is likely to be the larva of a tapeworm.

Cultured pearls are produced by introducing a foreign object into the flesh of an oyster, and obtaining the same results. That means that a true "cultured" pearl is an actual pearl, but it is less valuable because it is artificially induced. It's impossible to distinguish a good cultured pearl from a real one unless you can peer into its center, through the drill hole, and see the foreign object which, in most cases, has to be big enough not only to be seen but not to be removed by the drill hole. An instrument called the endoscope is used for this purpose, and it obviously entails milady removing her pearl necklace from her neck and then unstringing the pearls, which is not the most practical thing in the world for The Provident Loan Society or anyone else to do.

As a result, the legitimacy of genuine pearls must be taken somewhat upon faith by the Society, through knowledge of ownership. Even when that's not the case, pearl loans have had to be perhaps the most conservative of any collateral accepted, on the basis of the cost paid in a retail establishment as compared with the loan offered. There is good reason. The Society has probably suffered more losses proportionally upon pearl necklaces, where an overgenerous loan had been made, than on any other single type of jewelry. Sometimes at the auction sales we hardly could give them away.

Of course, the excellence of some cultured pearls, and even the abundance of pretty good "false pearls" (glass balls coated with freshwater fish scale) wreaks havoc with the pearl market. No one, except a real connoisseur of pearls, quite knows what he's doing, and this sort of audience is not likely to produce stable auction sale results.

The Pearl Story

In one of his short stories, P. G. Wodehouse described a situation as having all the somber gloom that pervades a Russian novel, or the smell of muddy shoes in a locked room. That is the way The Provident Loan Society felt about the pearl situation throughout the 1930's. Almost invariably, when a pearl item had to go to sale the results were at best very disappointing, and at worst catastrophic.

And we did get quite a few pearls. They are frequently not only a person's most valuable jewelry possession, but they obviously fitted the Society's definition of what was acceptable as a pledge: articles of value that are not too bulky, fragile, or perishable to be stored in the vaults. A potential borrower who had paid a juicy amount for a lovely pearl necklace was not going to think very highly of a supposedly public-service lender who wouldn't make him or her a loan on it, simply because the Society feared it didn't know enough to do so intelligently. We simply had to accept pearls as collateral. A couple of our specialist appraisers knew as much about them as almost anyone, but no one could rely upon the eventual market for them with anything like the confidence we had in evaluating diamonds, or even the colored precious stones. It was always a big gamble when, for one reason or the other, we made a substantial loan on pearls.

We were not the only people in those days to whom pearls

were a headache. Extremely good cultured pearls were flooding the market, for one thing, and even they were suffering from overproduction. Affairs reached a stage where a major producer of cultured pearls, Micky Moto, hit the front pages of newspapers all over the world by shoveling hundreds of thousands of his product into a furnace in order to satisfy people that he would not break the market any further than he had.

Two of the most prestigious Fifth Avenue jewelry stores got into different sorts of trouble because of their stake in pearls. One, which was thought to have the outstanding expert in the field—it was claimed he could distinguish a genuine pearl from a cultured one by the smell—would have failed had it not been able to merge with another distinguished house. The other great store became so upset about its discrimination that every pearl necklace in the establishment—and there were literally hundreds—was unstrung so that each pearl could be checked for its genuineness on an endoscope! What a job! To take arbitrary round numbers for simplicity of the mathematics, say they had 100 necklaces averaging fifty pearls each. That would have meant examining 5,000 pearls with the scrupulous care that an endoscope inspection demands.

The most remarkable example of the Society's problem in disposing of even very fine pearls in my day was the experience we had with a magnificent pearl rope. If worn as a single strand it would reach to a woman's knees, but I can't conceive of anyone except possibly a vamp of the silent films wearing it that way. Even Theda Bara or Pola Negri, on their way to Rudolph Valentino's tent in the desert, would be too likely to be caught by the heels and trip. But as a double, triple, or even quadruple set of strands, the rope became an absolutely stunning, if theatrical, piece.

It is breaking no confidentiality to tell you that these pearls belonged to a very interesting theatrical person—as a matter of fact, Anne Nichols, the author of the seemingly perpetual long-run stage hit, *Abie's Irish Rose.* The reason the ownership can be revealed is that during the course of the year that it took the Society to sell her pearls, Miss Nichols herself talked quite openly and freely to many dealers in an attempt to interest them, and each time the rope came up in one of the Silo auctions, the buzz around the room was punctuated with her name.

I cannot remember what Miss Nichols originally paid for the rope at a famous retail jewelers, but I know she produced her bill of sale when we made her loan. Since the Society loaned $3,500 on the article, I would guess that its original retail price probably was right around $20,000. If the Provident made a $3,500 loan, it was with the expectation that if the article went to sale it should bring perhaps $4,500, more or less, and those proportions of our wholesale levels, related to retail prices, was about right.

Miss Nichols did not redeem her piece, and in February 1939 it was offered at auction for the first time. The starting price, as was the usual practice, was the amount of the loan: $3,500. The auctioneer, after his preliminary extolling of the rarity and sumptousness of the rope, started his chatter, looking for this bid from someone.

For thirty seconds, except for the auctioneer's repetition of "$3,500, $3,500, who will give me $3,500?" a pin dropped in the midst of that audience would have made a deafening clatter. Then, without any marked enthusiasm, a dealer called out, "$3,000."

The Provident frequently had to be philosophical and accept a bid lower than the starting price when it thought nothing was to be gained by refusing it. That was when we felt we could do no better the following month. But in this case the decision was to stand firm, and the piece was passed. We thought that once the word got around among pearl men, who were not regular patrons of our sale, that a really fabulous pearl bargain would be coming up at a subsequent sale, we would at least get our asking price.

I was in charge of overseeing Silo's conduct of sales for The Provident Loan Society for three and a half years. In the course of that time many lots were passed for this sort of reason, but in every other case, after two or at most three subsequent failures to secure satisfactory bids, we gave up, dropped back the starting prices, and sold those articles at a loss. In the case of the Anne Nichols pearl rope, however, we were so convinced that at $3,000 we would be letting her prized possession go for the proverbial mess of pottage, that we hung on. And hung on. And hung on. For nine consecutive months we continued to try to start the bidding at $3,500 until, as the rope was held up each passing month only to be greeted by catcalls, hoots, and hysterical laughter that could be heard all the way from West 47th Street to the Bowery, this beautiful article had become the object of more derision than could be believed.

It was not so much that the Society was stupidly hardheaded about sticking to its guns. Private individuals would hear the background and would be assured that the dealers were refraining because most of them were not pearl-oriented and not because this wasn't a wonderful bargain. On several occasions during those embarrassing months, a private individual at the exhibitions would indicate that he or she was going to bid on the article when it came to sale. But although we on the auction dais were figuratively waiting on tiptoe to be kissed, the months passed and our prospective buyer always copped out.

At the end of nine months we really thought we had a valid purchaser for the rope. Quite an old lady had consulted a dealer that she trusted, and he had confirmed to her our statement that the purchase of the rope by anyone who wanted it (he happened not to) for less than $5,000 would be a very good investment. She spoke to me and told me that she thought she'd go as high as $4,500 if she had to do so. I reassured her that she was practically certain to secure the pearls, if that was the case, and that there was a strong likelihood that the lot would be knocked down to her at the starting price of $3,500. Would she care to leave that bid with the auctioneer, and only participate in the bidding in case it met with competition?

No, thank you. Bidding at a sale was the fun of it. She would act for herself.

Sure enough, the day came and my lady was sitting in the first row. When the lot was offered at a starting price of $3,500, and after the usual catcalls, silence once again reigned. Then one of the regular dealers called "$1,500!" in the most disparaging way such a sum can be called. I looked down from my seat at the lady and tried to make an encouraging signal to her, but she avoided my eye and sat like the sphinx. A minute of silence from the audience went by, and we had passed the lot again.

Later I asked her why she had not grasped the opportunity to buy the rope at a price considerably less than she had been satisfied it was worth. She replied that the $1,500 call had stopped her in her tracks. Had no one bid, she had been ready to offer the $3,500 starting price. But when she heard the $1,500 bid she had panicked completely and had wondered if she were not being a fool. Now, after talking once again to her dealer acquaintance and to me, she regretted her inaction, and we would see her again next month.

We never did see her again. When she didn't make an appearance on the tenth occasion that we had tried to sell the rope, we decided this had gone on long enough and that we had better drop the starting price, even though it would mean a big loss on the loan. Accordingly, we offered the rope for $3,000 when it next came up, this time to the accompaniment of raucous cheers from the crowd, which was thoroughly enjoying the whole long-strung-out affair. Cheers, but once again not a single bid. We were now worse off than we had been ten months previously when, at the time the pearls had first been offered, a dealer had been willing to pay $3,000. And at the normally excellent Christmas season sale, once again no bid was forthcoming.

Finally, *mirabele dictu,* there came the twelfth month, the January 1940 auction. A regular dealer customer of our auctions came to me on an exhibition day and said that he had convinced a private client of his that the rope was a steal at $3,000. We could enter a bid for him in the auctioneer's book. He did not want to bid himself from the floor because he didn't want to face the kidding he felt he would receive from his dealer friends and competitors for being the one who had finally gotten the Provident more or less off the hook. He felt the rope ought to be knocked down to him immediately for the $3,000 starting price, but if by some miracle there turned out to be some competitive interest, we could go as high as $3,750.

The bid was entered in the auctioneer's book, the lot was offered at $3,000, and the auctioneer indicated that he had obtained that figure. People looked around to see who was bidding, but of course they couldn't spot anyone. The auctioneer allowed another five or ten seconds to pass, in case a voice might descend from the mount. When none did, he finally put a merciful end to our traumatic experience by knocking the pearls down to our dealer friend for $3,000.

Over a full year, the Society had enough rope to hang itself. That is what I wrote in my monthly auction sales report to my bosses. Yet in the half-year that followed, three of the most solid and reputable dealers independently told me that they regretted not having bought the pearls at about the $3,500 level, when they had the chance. They simply had not known enough about the turnover market for pearls, and that is exactly why the Provident always was apprehensive about making pearl loans, particularly loans of any size. We didn't know enough either.

Is there a moral to this story? Only this, and it's a generalization about the pearl market as I knew it, not an absolute truth about the way things are today. Nonetheless, if when you bite into your next order of oysters on the half-shell you encounter a pearl, don't have dreams of being able to retire to Laguna Beach. It's more likely that if you could find enough pearls, in subsequent orders of oysters, to have a total value that would enable you to buy a bus ticket there, you wouldn't be able to lift the bag that contained them.

CHAPTER 7

Sold at Auction

One day in the autumn of 1938 I stepped out of the front door of the Provident Loan's Executive Office and into the chauffeur-driven long black limousine waiting for me. This marked the beginning of my most interesting and dramatic years with the Society. The chief operating officer, Arthur H. Ham, had appointed me to take charge of the auction sales, and had issued instructions that all necessary help and facilities I needed be furnished to me. My basic job of assisting Munroe Bates in running the Appraisal Department wasn't over, but I would only devote half my time to it from now on. For two weeks of every month I was to have a different assignment of my very own, where I was to be the boss.

The first week was to be spent traveling to each of our twenty-two offices, spread all over Greater New York City, to look over and verify the way the branch offices had listed the collateral coming up for sale. If I saw articles where the suggested starting price had been keyed to the loan, the usual practice, and I felt that any such starting levels and correlative expectations of auction sales prices were out of line, I was to change them. This could work in either direction. An old loan might have been made on jewelry on which fashions had changed and the market had declined, so that the original evaluation of worth was too high. Conversely, the Society's appraisers had no authority to lend excess amounts over the breakup value on articles, because of their beauty and workmanship. On such pieces, both the loan and the estimate of what we were likely to obtain at auction were often wildly too low.

By this time it was felt that I knew as much about such matters as anyone at the Provident, which was a point of view with which I wasn't inclined to disagree. This new job not only gave me immensely more responsibility and prestige, but it was obvious that it would be full of variety and fascination. What is more it carried a whopping big raise! I forget the exact figure, but I imagine it must have been something fantastic, like another $15 a week, and it brought me right into the luxury level of pay in those days: close to $100 a week. I was going to be rich beyond the dreams of avarice!

What was more, the perquisites were most attractive, and the first of them was that chauffeured limousine. The Society owned both the Cadillac and the chauffeur. I don't mean he was a slave, but at least he was on the permanent payroll without any other discernible function. I may be doing both the automobile and the driver an injustice, but no one ever quite knew why either existed in so rigidly economical an organization as the Provident. Their use seemed so minimal as to be almost nonexistent, and those were the days when taxicabs were plentiful and trying to capture *your* attention, rather than bowling merrily down the center of the avenue and studiously avoiding your frantic signals. So if something very special ever came up that called for one of us to ride in anything more magnificent than the IRT or a bus, a taxi would have appeared to have been the answer, even if the very thought of such unnecessary extravagance would have gone against the grain of the Provident's treasurer.

Still, for one mysterious and unknown reason or the other, that sumptuous limousine and that impeccable chauffeur did exist and were always on tap. Most of the time the chauffeur sat in a small anteroom reading the *Daily News* and occasionally trying his hand at its crossword puzzle. He certainly wasn't overworked. And so it came to pass that Mr. Ham, in his infinite wisdom, decreed that I was to have the use of the limousine and the driver for the one week in the month when I'd be visiting the branch offices.

In an era when very few people were in a position to travel around New York in the style of royalty, that limousine was like a panache in my hat. (Men wore hats then.) Waiting by the curb until I would finish in the Times Square office, the car would move quietly through the snow, rain, and slush as I emerged and whisk me off to the Penn Station office without my having to get my feet wet. (Parking for long periods at the curb was easier then.) Scheduling my arrival at the City Hall office or the Brooklyn office to coincide with the noon hour, I would lunch graciously at Fraunces Tavern or at Gage and Tollner's. (Restaurants were better then.)

There were twenty-two Provident Loan Society offices in 1938, tucked away in their elegance in every nook and corner of the great city. I came to know New York far better than any sightseer bus driver, because such buses merely drive past showy places. But we went everywhere and stopped for hours, during the course of which I usually could find time to reconnoiter the streets. Much of the time I was wandering through areas I had known before, or have seen since, but who except a local resident would ever think of visiting Hunts Point or Brownsville?

Twenty-two offices then, and only eight today, one of which is a new one. That means that fifteen of the branch offices I knew so well are gone, either sold and razed for new construction, or else converted into something so wildly different from a Provident office as to make me blink. Where are the snows of yesteryear? For that matter, where am I? Lost in digression, I'm afraid, but ready to return to the story.

The second of my two-week assignment each month on auction sales affairs took me to the auction rooms themselves. The better grade of jewelry was sent to the J. P. Silo Galleries, a huge, ground-floor establishment on the southwest corner of Vanderbilt Avenue and 45th Street, near Grand Central Station. Today it too is almost unrecognizable to me, for it now is a branch of the Manhattan Savings Bank. Like savings banks the countryside over, it usually serenely sits there festooned with potted palms. But on occasion its windows are jammed with casseroles and television sets, gifts to entice new depositors.

On such occasions, all those worldly goods might make one vaguely associate the present-day room with what it contained when the Provident was conducting a sale, but that would be the only connection. Silo's was a distinguished auction gallery, with a reputation in New York second only to Parke-Bernet for its wide variety of important sales. As far as jewelry was concerned, handling the Society's monthly sales established Silo's as the outstanding regular auction in that field, not only in the city but in the entire world. Distinguished and important Silo's was, but serene it was not. Exhibition days for private individuals were crowded and intense, exhibition days for dealers were frantic and furious, and actual sales days sometimes produced an atmosphere not unlike that of a major battle.

My role in all this, during the second week of my two-week stint, was rather like that of the Commissioner of Baseball. He is no one's boss, doesn't manage any team, and certainly is not called upon to be the pivot man in a double play. I had no connection with Silo's, had no personal stake in who bought what and for how much, and did not conduct any auctioneering. I was there as the Society's voice and conscience to see that Silo's ran the auction the way the Society demanded it be run. I was also there to inform and counsel private buyers, so that they could be on even terms during the auctions with their more sophisticated competitors, the jewelry merchants. Perhaps my posture was someplace between that of the Commissioner and an umpire.

Monday and Tuesday of each of those weeks were exhibition days for nondealers. Wednesday and Thursday were the dealer exhibition days. Friday and Saturday were the days of the actual sales. (Yes, Virginia, people worked five and a half or six days a week during the 1930's.)

The two exhibition days for the general public were the intensely busy ones for my assistant and me. For one thing, many more people attended the exhibition then than on dealer exhibition days. And almost everyone who was serious about buying anything wanted our information, advice, and even assistance in bidding. It is true that many people merely attended the exhibitions as a free form of entertainment, and a better one it was than a lot of museums, but out of the many hundreds who flocked to Silo's on those days, a substantial percentage intended to buy, and very few were at all knowledgeable about the merchandise. While Silo's was charged with the actual conduct of the exhibitions and sales, we of the Society were responsible for its overall supervision, and for offering our expertise to individuals who sought it. Almost without exception, all private buyers did; even one who knew quite a lot about an article could benefit hugely by consulting us.

I doubt if any salesmen in any other field ever were more open in the sharing of knowledge with potential customers. To cite an example, it was common practice for jewelry stores to describe their better quality diamonds as being blue-white in color. That was a term popularized in the advertisements of retail establishments, even though it has no gemological credibility, and most people thought it meant the finest color. The fact was that "blue-white" was used even by some big and reputable diamond stores for a range of color distinctions that could descend as far down as the third gradation on our diamond test sticks. To the casual eye, and certainly under something less than good light conditions, these were indeed diamonds of good color. But they embraced such a range that the poorest of them might not be worth any more than perhaps two-thirds of an identical stone of really fine color.

We were much more specific than any jewelry store in our conversations with private customers. We described our own grading system on diamond colors as frankly as has been done in a previous chapter of this book, and explained to the individual that although the diamond in which he was interested was indeed of excellent color, it was (let us say) no better than the second or third top gradation of the group we had established as standards. If this frankness made the potential buyer uneasy about its quality, we'd reassure him with the statistic, then accepted, that less than 3 percent of all diamonds on the market would qualify as falling into our top gradation of "Fine White," and even if his choice was ranked as a "Very Slightly Off" stone by us, it still would be among the top 20 percent of diamonds available, as far as its color was concerned.

With equal frankness and uncommonly detailed explanations, we'd give comparable information about the other factors that determine a diamond's worth: size, flaws, and excellence of cut or lack of excellence. We would then tell the interested party what the starting price would be when the article was first offered from the auctioneer's stand, and what our statistics indicated its probable final selling price would be. Along with that went the caution that the same information was being given to everyone else who inquired, so if the prospective buyer decided to get into the bidding, he or she should be prepared to top our estimate to some extent even though it well might not be necessary. If it was, however, a buyer at our sale who kept anywhere close to our sales estimate would surely be getting a bargain, because these were truly rock-bottom wholesale prices. Approximately 90 percent of the lots would be bought by dealers for eventual retail sale. After a gem had probably passed through several hands, with each wholesaler taking a profit, the final retail markup would be at least three times what was paid at the Society's auction, and might be considerably more.

All through the long hours of the public's exhibition days we were engaged in this type of discussion. The Silo attendants, standing behind long glass-topped counters in which the articles were displayed, handed them out one at a time, to be inspected and returned to the cases under the counter. That was their entire function, and queries were referred to my assistant and to me.

We were not incredible marvels at the art of instant appraisal. The necessary information was right at hand in the form of a card for each lot, filed by ascending lot numbers and stored in wooden boxes. Those were the cards that I had checked, verified, and sometimes altered during the preceding week, when I had made my tour of each of the offices to inspect at my leisure the collateral scheduled to be sold that month. Now, at the exhibition, I was able to pick out the appropriate card when a person inquired about a certain lot, glance at the description that was written on it, and go into my spiel with confidence that I knew what I was talking about.

If the customer could not be present at the sale, or possibly was nervous about competing in an auction against sophisticated professionals, he or she could leave a bid with me and I would enter it in the auctioneer's catalogue to be used by him as far as became necessary. In other words, I might tell a person that a ring would first be offered for $100, that the bidding would advance first in $10 jumps and then probably slide off to $5 and even $2.50 additional increments, and that we thought it would probably fetch around $140 in the end. I might advise leaving a $150 bid, or suggest $155, just to top someone else who might decide to go to $150 and quit. I assured such a person that if the bidding never reached that level but, let us say, all offers from the floor has ceased at $125, then the auctioneer would call out no more than the minimum topping bid at that point for the benefit of the bidder marked in his catalogue. If there was no further bidding, he would knock the piece down to the private buyer for $130. One could leave a bid with us for any amount at all, perhaps wildly in excess of our estimates, and it positively would not be used except to top a competing bid by the minimum amount.

I once received a bid of this type for $1,050 from a knowledgeable customer who felt we had badly underestimated the potential sales value of an emerald that we were quoting as likely to sell for $400. He thought it might bring as much as $1,000, and added the extra $50 as a safeguard. His bid was entered in the catalogue, and the article was started at $300. (No lifting of the starting price, either, just because a high bid was in our hands.) He was right—the emerald did fetch more than $400, but only because he was bidding. Without his entry in the catalogue, it would have been knocked down to a dealer for $375. After hearing that bid, the auctioneer called "$400" for the private bidder, and then this last competing dealer offered $410. The auctioneer chanted, "$420, 420, 420 . . . ," and after another moment's pause let his hammer fall.

The two dealer exhibition days were very different from the public days. With the much smaller attendance, but one consisting of men who were examining just about every article scheduled to be sold, the Silo staff had a much harder time of it and we, of the Provident, a much easier one. About fifteen or twenty small tables with chairs were set up and reserved for the jewelry traders who had run up the biggest bills at the most recent auctions. These major customers were allowed to take a whole tray of articles at a time to their respective tables, and retain it while they examined each piece and marked their catalogues for those items in which they were interested. No fixed time limit was imposed for how long they could keep a tray, but the pressure of having to cover the entire huge stock in so short a period as two working days guaranteed that no one would retain one excessively long. When a man had finished his work on a tray, he would return it to the Silo attendant who had checked it out to him, and take another. And so, working methodically throughout the two days, the big operators would quite literally mark just about every item, each with his own secret code as far as his price evaluation was concerned—in case his catalogue was lost or stolen, and fell into the hands of a rival dealer.

My assistant and I were once again available for information and consultation, but the important dealers as a rule were too proud to seek advice. Generally their questions were confined to how many stones were mounted in an elaborate diamond article, such as a wide bracelet, to save them making a count. Or what amount we intended to start the piece at when it was first offered. Or one might tell us he thought a gold or silver article had been improperly stamped by the manufacturer and might be a fraud, and had we been struck by the same idea?

We were under no more constraint in answering all dealer questions to the best of our ability than we were with private people. The big difference was that this sort of dealer was usually either too sophisticated or too reserved to ask a great number of questions.

The less important dealers, whose interest ran only to a few scattered articles each, were handled on dealer days exactly the way private individuals were handled on their exhibition days. Silo attendants checked out one article at a time to them, and they stood by the counter, or near the windows if they wanted to see color better, without benefit of a table or chair. Such men were much more likely to solicit our advice and opinion. And, whenever asked, we gave it.

The dealers, frequently suspicious and sometimes almost violently antagonistic to each other, trusted the integrity of the Society's sales to a sometimes remarkable degree. On one occasion, the dealer who invariably purchased more articles in our sales, month after month, than anyone else, knew that he wouldn't be able to be present. He spent the two dealer days marking up his catalogue, with an entry opposite almost every lot number. Instead of assigning the bidding to an associate, he turned over the catalogue to me and asked us to handle it for him. (This time he had written his bids conventionally, and we did not have to call in deciphering experts to break his code.) We managed to buy just as much as he usually obtained when he was present himself, and at what he later told me was right in line with his price determinations. He would usually buy something over 100 articles at each sale, after having appraised several hundred at the exhibition, and his total bill for a sale was likely to be somewhat in excess of $10,000. There were two reasons why he would only be able to secure a fraction of the articles in which he was interested. The first was the heavy withdrawal of many lots that had been scheduled for sale, catalogued, and exhibited, but which never did reach the auction stand. This was the result of last-minute renewals or redemptions by the pledgers. All through sales week, and sometimes even minutes before an article was to go on the block, our telephone would ring and the news was flashed to us that lot number such-and-such should be taken out of the sale because the interest on the loan had just been paid in the local office. The second reason was the natural one—that he was outbid on some of the pieces he wanted. However, almost like clockwork, this particular dealer did pick up his 100 purchases or so for about $10,000, and that month when he left all his bidding to us, the results were almost identical. It must have been a temptation to him from then on to do the same thing again, take the sales days off, and go to the ball game.

As an example of the integrity of operation, that episode is interesting. But it called for nothing on our part except honesty and careful clerical performance. It was an unusually large routine performance, but no more than that.

Quite another and much more spectacular sort of reliance upon the Society's auction cropped up one morning during the exhibition for private individuals. A very well-dressed stranger came to me at my desk and introduced himself. His name meant nothing to me, but his business card indicated that he was president of one of the city's major banks. He told me that he knew nothing at all about jewelry but had heard that the Provident's sales offered good opportunities to buy gems at bargain prices. He was looking for ways to diversify his assets. Because the possession of jewelry has historically seemed to be a good thing in difficult financial periods, he thought he might dip his toe into those waters. What did I think? Did we have anything that I believed might be a good investment?

The outstanding characteristics that I felt should exist for ideal investment in this field were threefold. First, the potential investor should buy a diamond and not any other precious stone, because the diamond market was a constant and busy one compared to that in emeralds, sapphires, or rubies, and that activity guaranteed much greater liquidity. Second, he or she should concentrate on nothing but truly fine diamonds of top quality color, flawless or very nearly so, and perfectly cut. Finally, the size of the diamond should make it an important and expensive possession, but not so large that its cost would limit possible resale to the extremely wealthy only. That meant that I was recommending something like a 3-carat diamond of gem quality, if we could find one in this sale.

There happened to be two such stones on exhibit, very similar to each other. One was a bit over 3 carats and had a barely discernible and unimportant flaw. The other was just under 3 carats and was perfect. Both were Fine White, and our quotation about expected prices was the same on each— $1,200. (Today it would be eight or ten times that much.)

I showed both rings to the man, explained their characteristics and why I thought them the best choices for him, and said I didn't feel it really mattered which one he might get. He replied that he didn't care either, as long as they were equally good investments, and what did I recommend? I suggested that he leave "if" bids on both, meaning that if his bid was successful on the first one to be sold, his bid on the second would be dropped. If he failed to get the first, his bid on the second would be in force. Also, I thought that the two bids on separate items would be a good idea in view of the very real chance that one or the other of the rings might be withdrawn before the sale, by reason of loan renewal or redemption. For his sake, we would hope that both would not be withdrawn. Finally, I pointed out that I'd been quoting those same $1,200 estimates to anyone else who was interested, and that he probably should leave us bids somewhat in excess of that figure.

He listened gravely, nodded, and left me the "if" bids, each for $1,300. He did not attend the sale himself. When the first of the two lots was offered—the larger stone with the slight flaw—I was able to secure it for him for $1,225. His $1,300 "if" bid on the other diamond was struck from the auctioneer's catalogue and, just to complete the incident although it has nothing to do with the story, that diamond was bought by a dealer for $1,250.

The man came in to Silo's the following Monday, paid his bill in cash, gravely thanked me, and went out onto East 45th Street to head wherever bank presidents go.

The following month he returned on one of the exhibition days, looked more or less casually at the four articles I thought the best recommendations for his purpose, and left bids on all four. One article was withdrawn before the sale and he was outbid on another, but we were able to buy the other two for him. He appeared again on the next Monday, peeled off twenty or thirty $100 notes from the roll he carried in his trouser pocket (without making the roll appreciably smaller), slipped his two new rings in his fob pocket, and wandered off again, puffing a pipe contentedly.

Then came the day, a month later, when he came to my desk on the first exhibition day and asked if we could go somewhere to talk to each other privately. I left the desk in my assistant's charge and took him into Mrs. Silo's private office.

"I'm convinced," he said, this time lighting up a panetela cigar. "I've had the jewelry you bought for me appraised, and it's clear that I've made extremely good buys. I've known of The Provident Loan Society's reputation for a long time, but I didn't have any knowledge of these auctions, run by a professional auction house. Most auctions, you know, are not exactly above suspicion, and since I was completely ignorant about jewelry, I didn't want to become a lamb among the wolves.

"But now I've watched the way things are run here, and I realize that you make sure the sales are handled the way the Provident does everything else. I trust the Society, and now I trust you. Everything up to now has just been an experiment to convince myself that this particular spreading of my eggs into other baskets is a good idea. I'm sold on it now.

"So go ahead this month and in the months to come, buy me more jewelry. I don't even want to see it until I come in to pick it up after the sales. Just buy anything that you think is a good investment for me. It doesn't have to be diamonds, it need not be rings, I don't care. I have no interest at all in jewelry as jewelry. I just want to put my money into it at this time. There's no limit on how many pieces you are to buy, or what you have to spend for them. Just buy whatever you think an attractive speculation, and don't quit until I tell you."

On this basis, for something like an entire year, I placed bids for this man on practically every article of gem quality that appeared in our sales, and spontaneously slipped bids in from the stand when something came along, which I hadn't chosen previously, but which I could see wasn't bringing the price it was worth. I ventured on occasion into colored precious stones, superb gold or silver articles, and once even bought a magnificent pearl necklace for him where I knew a cabal of the pearl dealers had conspired not to bid against each other, so that one of them could purchase it cheaply for the group. The unexpected competition from my secret bidder panicked the dealer representative, who had no chance to consult his colleagues as to how much higher he could go, and my private buyer secured a marvelous pearl necklace for a fire-sale price.

In that particular year the Society's auction sales were the biggest in its history. In normal times less than 2 percent of loans are forfeited and have to go to the auction rooms. But during the Depression, when people needed money so desperately and the loan balance was at its peak (in the neighborhood of close to $40 million), a greater percentage went unredeemed or unrenewed, and something nearer 8 percent of loans went to sale. That meant we had to have very big sales indeed every month. In a couple of those Depression years, including the one in which this story takes place, the auctions grossed approximately a couple of million dollars, and that was when a dollar really *was* a dollar. The retail value at that time would have been between $5 and $10 million—and, at a guess, would today be nearer $25 million.

That's a lot of ice! And my man had unobtrusively picked up the cream of it, to mix a metaphor. On the appropriate Monday of each month, he duly showed up at Silo's equipped with a checkbook and a briefcase, for his many purchases couldn't be handled as cavalierly as in the first couple of months. And then, almost twelve months to the day after I had first seen him, he paid his final bill and said to me, "That's all."

I have no way of checking what his total purchases were over that year, but I remember they ran into several hundreds of thousands of dollars, and that their retail worth must have been well over $1 million. If he is alive and still has them all, I'd wager their retail value now would be something like $5 million. As far as investments go, I don't imagine he would have done much if any better with Polaroid when that stock was making headlines, and he'd certainly be better off today.

"And now," he said, lighting the pipe to which he had switched back, "what can I do for you?"

"Why nothing, thank you. Nothing. It was just my job."

"Come off it. It may have resembled your job, but in magnitude and exercise of your personal judgment it was a hell of a lot more. You did it for me, and I owe you a commission."

I did a bit of fast mental arithmetic. Any commission at all—even one percent on the approximate half-million dollars of purchases he had rolled up—would be more than my salary for a year, at that time. For that matter, what sort of percentage was meant by "a commission"? Two percent? *Five* percent? TEN percent?

Get thee behind me, Satan.

"I'm sorry, I really can't take anything from you. I work for the Provident and it has its own very rigid ideas about what employees can do and what they absolutely can't do. Taking a commission very definitely would fall into category two. If it were ever known, I'd be fired, and I don't want to be fired. I think I'm in line to head up the Society one of these days, and I don't want either to queer it or have it on my conscience, much as I could use some extra money. No, thanks."

"I never heard anything more ridiculous. You've done something special and extraordinary for me for a long time, and I'm grateful. It would be absurd if the Society wouldn't let you accept a gift from me."

"Absurd or not, and I'm not at all sure I agree with you, the Provident would throw me out on my ear. No again, but thank you *very* much."

"Well, suppose you buy some things and have the bills sent to me? Or why don't you take the sort of trip you can't afford on your vacation this year, and let me pay the entire freight?"

"I simply can't. Or rather, won't."

"Well, damn it, I can't force you. All right, forget it. But I'll tell you what. I know you're a keen tennis player. Have you ever seen court tennis? You know, the royal game that originated in Florence and which the Kings of England played at Hampton Court? It's a marvelous game, and there are only a couple of courts in the East. One of them is in the Racquet Club, just a few blocks away. Would you like to have lunch with me there, and put on some tennis clothes I have in my locker, and I'll show you the game?"

Of course I knew vaguely about that mysterious game of court tennis, which was played exclusively by millionaire sportsmen. It was a temptation for so keen a tennis bug as I, and I decided that even the implacable dictums of the Provident Loan could be relaxed to this extent. If Mr. James Speyer were looking down from heaven, he might even smile gently.

I accepted. We had a fine lunch and, after half an hour of practice at the baffling game, I even was able to give him a decent contest. I had a splendid time, and that was my commission.

I did not use this gentleman's bank, and I never saw him again.

If the reader feels that the foregoing is an almost incredibly unrealistic story, smacking of a self-righteous piety that is almost stomach-turning, I could not blame you. But I would suspect you are under forty and that your opinions are conditioned by those affairs you have seen or experienced, from political kickbacks and smart income tax evasion techniques, to the 1970's climate of Watergate. I would ask the young reader to remember that forty years ago we all still had something of the Horatio Alger, Jr., ideal of success, in which hard, steady, honest toil was the only right road that could take one from rags to riches. I hear voices: "Horatio Alger, Jr. Who's he?"

CHAPTER 8

Curiouser and Curiouser

Not all of the Society's unredeemed collateral went to the Silo auction rooms for sale. The items that had very little appeal for private buyers, and were essentially only of interest to dealers for the broken-up and melted-down U.S. assay price obtainable for precious metals, were sent to the Shongut auction rooms in the Bowery. This practice of dividing each month's goods into two separate sales benefited each. Neither sale had to run over the course of several days, which would have been necessary if everything had been combined into one auction. The attractive and expensive items were sold uptown at Silo's, located in a part of town that made it accessible not only to private individuals of means, but also to the elite of the dealers on West 47th Street. The other items, consisting chiefly of gold chains, old-fashioned watches that no one would want for use but whose gold cases were substantial and valuable, unattractive silverware that shrieked to be melted down and fabricated into something better, and other articles of that sort, went to Shongut's. The dealers whose establishments remained downtown in the Bowery, once the heart of the trade, were for the most part those who had not been able to make the move up to West 47th Street, where the more prosperous dealers had gone to expose themselves to more affluent customers.

My own responsibilities were focused completely upon the sales at Silo's, but I visited the Shongut sales on several occasions, my justification being that I was checking that all was going well there. It invariably was. And since the items on sale were so routine, and the method of selling so fixed in traditional technique, supervision by the Provident Loan wasn't required. The fact of the matter is that I was fascinated by what went on during the sales at Shongut's, and wanted to witness a few of them as a form of entertainment.

As a rule there only were about ten or a dozen dealers who competed for the goods offered at these auctions, and no private buyers at all. The auctions were not closed to the public, and indeed it's the law that pawnshop auction sales must be announced in a newspaper public notice. But an ordinary person, wandering into Shongut's with the idea of picking up something at sale, would have been as frustrated as a five-foot basketball player being tossed into a professional game.

The auctioneer perched on an ordinary wooden chair, set upon a very small, square platform that raised him about a foot above floor level. Seated around the platform were the ten to twelve dealers who were participating in the auction, and each established his position with the auctioneer prior to the sale and laid claim to some portion of his clothing or anatomy. One would have a finger on the toe of the auctioneer's left shoe, another on his thigh, one in the small of his back or pinching his elbow. The only thing that might have stopped a latecomer, who couldn't find any unstaked terri-

tory, from goosing him, was the fact that the auctioneer was
seated.

Why? Well, since each of these merchants knew exactly as
much as the others about what the assay price of each article
was, open bidding simply would not have worked. Fourteen-
karat gold, for instance, is worth so much per pennyweight.
If one determines that a gold chain *is* 14K and then weighs
it, a simple multiplication tells the established price that can
be obtained for it. So the distinctions between what one
dealer might be willing to pay for that chain, and what another would, rested almost completely upon tiny discoveries
each might unearth. Did it have brass clips at its ends, or bits
of solder to strengthen certain links? That might have been
responsible for a pennyweight on the scales, and should be
deducted. Did the acid test show that the chain, although
marked 14K, actually seemed closer to 13K—or 15K? Change
one's intended bid down, or up, accordingly.

Yet, in the end, the base price of gold or silver is so fixed
at any one time that every dealer would be marking his catalogue very much the same as anyone else. The variations in
their estimates often came down to that chain, for example,
actually being worth $23.37 in assay value, so if a dealer
marked it for $23.25 he had done well: if he decided on
$23.50 he had goofed.

Profits and losses in pennies don't seem terribly critical
today, when a man is likely to toss pennies out of his trouser
pocket because they make him lopsided, but even pennies
were a respectable form of currency during the Depression.
One of them would buy you stick of gum or a small piece of
candy. Two were enough to pick up your morning *Daily
News, World,* or *The New York Times.* (At that, the price of

the *Times* had skyrocketed since World War I, when it had been one cent.) Five cents got you a seat on the trolley or the subway. Dealers at the Bowery sales were able to buy in quantity, since there was so much spread among so few, and they were glad to make profits in pennies. If they successfully obtained enough articles that could turn even a small profit apiece for them, they had put in a good day's work.

Thus the trouble with open bidding was that a number of competitors would be sure to shout out the same bid simultaneously, and probably the correct one that would assure some profit. At best, that put the auctioneer in an impossible situation. At worst, it precipitated a free-for-all fistfight. So, instead, the auctioneer sat stolidly on his chair, staring straight ahead, and chanted the bids as he felt each prod or pinch: "Nineteen and one-half, nineteen and three-quarters," and so on until what seemed like his exquisite torture ceased, and he announced that Dealer Greene, who had latched onto his right kneecap, was the successful bidder. The system may well have given rise to injustices at times, but it did have one great virtue. There could be no arguing about the speed with which the auctioneer's motor reactions varied in transmitting impulses from his kneecap to his brain, as opposed to those emanating from his ankle, and if he said that Greene's tweak took the piece, Greene got it.

Because prices at Shongut's almost invariably were geared to the value of the metal and nothing more, which was also the factor upon which the loans on the articles had been based, most lots realized just about what was expected of them, and substantial surplus amounts for the borrower were rare. Almost without exception, the bonanza windfall of a fat surplus came from the Silo sales, but now and then something surprising could transpire at Shongut's as well. This could happen when one of the many Provident office appraisers, making the conservative value-of-the-metal appraisal that was all he was authorized to offer as a loan, failed to note that the article had extra attractions when he later described it for auction sales purposes. Similarly we, who checked the auction sale cards, could either overlook such a feature or be unaware of it. The result was that on rare occasions some article that should have been sent to Silo's, where more knowledgeable and sophisticated buyers would have recognized the unobvious, were routinely sent to Shongut's. I have related how this almost happened in "The Sapphire Story" in a previous chapter. In that case, with no suspicion that the "blue stone" was a genuine sapphire, and no instruments to establish its authentic characteristics, there is little doubt that the pendant would have been sold for next to nothing to a dealer, who might never have known what he had in his possession before disposing of it elsewhere.

Jacob Shongut Inc., Auctioneers, still operates, along with the other major Bowery establishment of the same nature, the Jewelry Auction Market of America. They are only a few doors away from each other, and between them they sell all the unredeemed loans of every commercial pawnshop in the city. Although their auctions are open to anyone who cares to attend or participate, virtually no one who is not a jewelry dealer ever does. The style of conducting such auctions is more conventional today than the one I witnessed so long ago, but the pace is too fast and the techniques too professional for anyone but the experienced merchant. It certainly was back then, too.

We did pull out of the Shongut sale exceptional looking

items of gold, or silverware, or good-looking modern watches in working order, or interesting articles we suspected might fall into the category of antiques, and we would then put them in the Silo sales. Even so, often we had no idea of what their real worth was. One time a very attractive but not particularly heavy silver water pitcher had been pledged in one of the offices for $3, which is what the per ounce weight of it justified at the time. Unredeemed after a year, the pitcher did indeed seem attractive enough to justify being put into the Silo sale rather than the Shongut one. When we were asked about its probable sales price, we said it might bring anywhere from $25 to $50, even though a $3 silver loan was generally not expected to realize more than about five dollars, or at most ten. It turned out that despite our generous quotation, we slightly underrated that pitcher.

More than one connoisseur was knowledgeable enough about silver to see that this was an authentic and extremely fine Paul Revere pitcher, a prime example of that great early American silversmith's best work. The word even got around to Henry Ford, who sent an agent to the auction to try to secure the pitcher for his museum at Dearborn. But the successful bidder was a dealer. He finally had it knocked down to him, after some of the wildest bidding ever seen at Silo's (the starting price was $20), for $2,200!

The Provident made its computations the following week, and sent a letter to the pledger of record, saying that upon presentation of her loan ticket, she would receive a surplus of $2,196.64 on her $3 loan. The letter came back stamped "addressee unknown," and so did subsequent follow-up letters. The woman who had pledged the pitcher was never found and, as happens in such cases, after a period of time the surplus was turned over to the State of New York. She could have come forward years later with her claim, and the State would have honored it. It still will.

Another time, a gold article was booked into the Silo sale which, it turned out, would have fared just as well at Shongut's, and caused less embarrassment. We were faced with something that didn't seem to be any article of adornment anyone had ever seen before, nor did there appear to be any way of wearing it. It was shaped rather like a very large staple with a head and two prongs, such as is used to hold together a sheaf of papers. The head was large enough that our only guess was that it might conceivably be a button, but securing so valuable a button by nothing but spread prongs did not seem a very realistic proposition. And valuable it was, for this thing, whatever it may or may not have been, was not the conventional 14K or 18K, but was undeniably 22-karat gold, which is very nearly pure gold. On that basis alone, since gold of that karatage is encountered so seldom, we felt it belonged at Silo's. Not knowing how to describe it, it was simply catalogued as "Gold object, 22K, 8 dwt (pennyweight)."

It lay in its tray at the public exhibition for half a day. I received a few inquiries about it, and what it was. I didn't have the foggiest idea and admitted it, feebly advancing the button theory but without much conviction. That afternoon, a regular private patron of the auctions whom I knew, a Park Avenue physician, approached me and asked me if I knew what the article was. I confessed I didn't. He said he did, although he had never seen one like it before. It was an early contraceptive device, used in harems in years past by Far Eastern royalty.

Armed with this new information, I decided to pick and choose which of the subsequent inquiries at the exhibition I would answer honestly from then on. There were certainly many to whom the button theory would be more palatable. In the end, it didn't matter very much. The dealers bid just as much as eight pennyweight of 22K gold was worth, and no more. My doctor friend picked up the "gold object" as a curiosity by calling one topping bid over that figure. The maharaja, or whoever had pledged the article, didn't get much of a surplus.

On the other hand, the Provident made a loan at one time on a dangling, gold, two-inch watch fob, at the end of which was encased a flat-topped emerald. Although a fairly good color, the emerald wasn't rated very highly by the appraiser who took it in, since it probably could not be used effectively in any other way than its present setting, and how many people would want a watch fob of this sort in the first place? He wrote out a loan for $12, chiefly predicated on the gold content of the article, and eventually it went to sale.

This did not happen in my time, so I do not know who recognized that the carving on the emerald was the old Imperial Russian crest, and that the fob had a history of being used by the czars to emboss the sealing wax on letters and documents. How did it get to The Provident Loan Society, and who pledged it? My informants, who still work for the Society, could not tell me, for it happened years before they joined the Society too. Perhaps it was handed down legitimately after White Russian families fled the revolution. Perhaps it was ripped off. In any event, the story of its history was bruited around the auction rooms sufficiently before the sale that the fob commanded a final bid in excess of $1,500.

Without knowing the number of the loan, and the office in which it was pledged, trying to track down who received the giant surplus is quite impractical today. Although the incident is vouched for as being true, only the general story has been handed down almost as legend, and the details that would make it complete are lost.

A recent pledge of similar nature, which was resolved in a different way, involved a dowager lady of society and a Finast supermarket delivery boy. When the lady was in her eighties and her entire family had left the nest, the nest being a baronial estate on the south shore of Long Island, she moved into a small Park Avenue apartment in New York. There she telephoned her grocery orders to a neighboring Finast store, and the same teenage boy delivered it each day. This went on for some years before the lady finally died.

In her will she bequeathed a Provident Loan Society ticket to the boy. Since such tickets are as negotiable as cash, that meant she had left him whatever was stored in the Provident's vaults under the loan number. The boy came to the Society office to try to find out if he had anything that was worth very much. The local office representative opened one or two of the very substantial number of packages that were stored under that loan and reported back to the boy that the loan had been made on thirty-six pieces of silverware, weighing a total of so many ounces, and that a loan in the hundreds of dollars had been tendered on it. He said that the silver he had seen looked to be very fine indeed, and that the value of the entire assortment might well be greatly in excess of the loan. He told the boy that if he couldn't redeem the loan, or didn't want to, the silver would be put up for auction eventually and that he would receive any surplus, but that wouldn't happen for the better part of another year.

The word "auction" gave the boy an idea. His Finast store was located not too far from the Southeby-Parke Bernet galleries, whose reputation he knew as the most prestigious of New York City auction rooms. He approached their silver department, displayed the Provident ticket and told his story, and asked if they might be interested in redeeming the silver for him and then, if it seemed worthwhile, selling it at one of their auction sales. If that could be done, he wouldn't have to wait such a long time before the Provident Loan auction would come up.

Southeby-Parke Bernet knew all about The Provident Loan Society, of course, and was conscious of the fact that any silverware on which the Society had loaned hundreds of dollars was of a nature that would almost surely bring one thousand dollars or more at one of their silver auctions. It did seem worthwhile as described. And if upon inspection of the silver it did not seem reasonable, it could all be put right back with the Society with the situation unchanged. "Let's go!" was their attitude.

It turned out to be one of the wiser moves of the decade for the boy. When the thirty-six articles were unwrapped and spread before the eyes of the gallery's experts, those eyes almost popped out of their sockets. The articles were a mixture of the finest type of English and Continental silverware. Among them were four pieces of Luigi Valdier, the last great 18th-century Roman artist-goldsmith, whose work has almost never been seen on the American market. As a silversmith he could be compared to the giant in English silver, Paul de

Lamerie, and he also executed and cast the bronze bell for St. Peter's while he was the official silversmith to the Vatican.

A Valdier oval serving dish, with two small plates, brought $7,500 when Southeby-Parke Bernet offered it in 1973. A rare two-handled silver gilt tray was purchased by a New Jersey silvermith for $8,500—more than twice the optimistic estimate put upon it prior to the sale. Altogether, the sale of the boy's silver realized approximately $40,000! With all due respect to the Provident's auction sales, it's doubtful if any such figure would have been obtained had the collateral pursued its normal course and been sold there. Even with the Southeby-Parke Bernet commission deducted, the boy had taken a spectacularly wise course of action. Whether he followed it up equally wisely is unknown. Perhaps he went to Harvard, perhaps he bought a Rolls-Royce. And perhaps he continued to deliver groceries, keeping his eyes open for another little old lady.

*

CHAPTER 9

The Distant Drum

The Aspirin Age eventually culminated in World War II. As the Thirties ended and the new decade began, the holocaust of that era in Europe sparked a number of minor echoes with us in New York.

First of all came the influx of refugees, fleeing their native lands and unable to bring along anything more than they could carry. As the war clouds grew blacker, many of the more farsighted divested themselves of their homes and other possessions and used the money to buy jewels. A steady flow of these unfortunate and desperate people came to the Provident's offices daily at that time, pledging their diamonds or gold, or whatever, to survive until they could make a place for themselves in their new country.

The strangest case of the use of the word "whatever," as far as the type collateral we were offered is concerned, had to do with a man from Holland. Originally from Germany, he became an immensely successful naturalized Dutch citizen after World War I, managing five companies in a tobacco syndicate in the Far East, and serving as a Rath Councillor to the Queen of Holland.

When World War II broke out he received notice from the Nazis to return to Germany and serve the Third Reich. He disregarded the notice, and knew he had to act if he were to salvage the personal possessions he prized most, his magnificent collection of paintings. He entrusted the most valuable of them to his son and daughter, instructing them to store the huge paintings with a European office of the American Express Company, until he could issue further instructions, and then to go to the United States and wait until he could join them.

Finally he did make his own way to New York, was reunited with his family, and managed to get the paintings across the Atlantic and into his possession. They consisted chiefly of Rembrandts and other Dutch masters of that period and later. He wanted to borrow a very substantial sum of money on them to establish himself in some sort of business here, and when he poured out his story to a branch office appraiser, he was referred to Munroe Bates at the Executive Office.

Munroe was impressed with the man and agreed to go with him to the modest boarding house, where he had taken a single room, and look at the paintings. They would be accompanied by the expert on art who appraised paintings for Silo's. So far so good. But when they arrived, Munroe and the expert were completely unprepared for what greeted their eyes as the door was opened to them.

In a room no larger than about twelve by fifteen feet, a bed, a bureau, and a chair were squeezed into an area completely filled with oil paintings. But the *size* of those oil paintings! No one of them measured any less than approximately seven feet by ten feet, and many were considerably larger. Rembrandts and other masters' works they were—the Silo expert verified their authenticity. But who, except a museum, could or would buy them? The day of the grand house had practically disappeared, and how many apartments had sufficient wall space to accommodate paintings of these dimensions? They would have made wonderful acquisitions for a bevy of beer barons, for their castles on the Rhine, but Silo's didn't have many customers at their paintings auctions who were beer barons, or who lived that way. No, said the expert, he would not advise our making a substantial loan on this collateral even if, as was doubtful, we felt we wanted to make room to store them. We did not.

A few days later the man came back to see Munroe with two small paintings, executed on wood. These, he claimed, were also by Rembrandt, and portrayed the artist's mother and father. Originally they had been one painting on one piece of wood, which had been broken apart at a later date. When Munroe put the two pieces of wood together, he could see from the join that this was almost surely true. At least there was a virtue in the one painting having been separated into two, from the Society's standpoint: Neither was of any size that would pose a storage complication.

The owner of an art gallery in the East Fifties was called in for consultation, and he was greatly impressed. He wouldn't swear to it on a Bible, but he felt they were genuine Rembrandts. Munroe and the owner then went to the Metropolitan Museum of Art to show the paintings to the curator, who expressed his regrets but said that he was not allowed to make appraisals for outsiders. He did, however, show the two men into the Rembrandt room and, after comparing brush strokes, ventured his strictly unofficial but favorable opinion about the paintings having been executed by Rembrandt.

Encouraged by the unanimity of the experts' judgments, Munroe agreed to extend enough of a loan to tide the man over a sufficient time until he could get adjusted and find work. Munroe did not feel the Society should take a chance on making a larger loan than the amount required for that. The sum of $1,500 was finally agreed upon and, with mixed emotions, the man accepted it if he could also have a certain privilege. Might a few art dealers view the paintings at the office? His real aim was to sell them, he explained. This courtesy was extended to him, and a short time later one of the dealers agreed to redeem the paintings and sell them for his own and the owner's joint benefit. Subsequently he succeeded in getting a five-figure sum for them.

The Chief Operations Officer of the Society, at that time, had heard about the whole affair and, before the paintings were redeemed, had asked to see them. He had not been wildly impressed, his own taste running more to Norman Rockwell, and when he learned of the eventual sales price he commented, "Those were the most expensive shingles I ever saw!"

During these years The Provident Loan Society was called upon frequently to finance travelers other than refugees from across the Atlantic. England imposed very strict restrictions on how much money a Britisher could take out of the country when he or she went abroad, whether on business or for pleasure. A limit of about $100 in cash was all that was permitted to an individual, and unless such a person had some other credit or exchange arrangement that legitimately, or otherwise, could pay United States bills, that sort of sum wouldn't go very far even on a brief vacation trip. Certainly one couldn't stay at the Plaza Hotel, or dine at "21," or take a look at California, to say nothing of doing any shopping more ambitious than in F. W. Woolworth's.

So it was not a rare sight to see a bowler-hatted gentleman, dressed in Savile Row flannels or tweeds and carrying the inevitable tightly furled umbrella, laying down the family jewels on the counter of a midtown branch office and inquiring, in a gentle South London accent, what he could raise on them. Consideration for the family's privacy precludes my telling the names of a certain married couple who took advantage of the Society's facilities more than once. They were quite close relatives of the Royal Family itself, and the sums they borrowed were sufficient to keep them in the style to which they were accustomed, while they were visiting. And somehow or other, their jewelry was always redeemed and available to be offered again the next time they came over. Rank hath its privileges.

Along about this time the Society made the largest loan it ever extended. It too was made by a foreigner, although not in connection with anything that had to do with the war. But 1939 was the year of New York's first World Fair, and one of the most spectacular exhibits was the House of Jewels, staged by the DeBeers Syndicate. Included in the display was a truly fabulous collection primarily composed of diamond, emerald, and ruby gems from China.

I would very much doubt the existence elsewhere of such an abundance of comparable jewelry owned by one individual. Obviously there are a number of cases where the possession of one of the fabled huge gemstones of history, such as the Cullinan diamond or the Kohinoor, the Orloff or the Pitt, cost the proud purchaser more than any batch of unknown and variegated jewelry, no matter how fine. All that I mean to imply is that every article in this Chinese collection combined, to an extent we had never seen before, the two basic characteristics of superb jewelry: craftsmanship and design of surpassing beauty, and absolutely top quality of gems in every aspect. The most outstanding jewelers in the world, such as Tiffany or Cartier or Harry Winston, might well never have had any such number of incredibly magnificent pieces of jewelry in their respective showcases at any one time.

There were great single-stone solitaire rings—diamonds, emeralds, rubies, and sapphires—flanked by baguette diamonds in most cases, and each could be used as a standard for the finest of its type. None of these solitaires was of the huge size that characterizes the historic stones cited above, those being 100 carats or more in weight, but gems of that size really have no functional use as jewelry that a woman can wear. The Kohinoor, for example, is in a display case in England along with the other Crown Jewels, and that's the sort of place where it belongs. It's not a thing the Queen would be likely to slip on for even the most distinguished and glamorous social affair. The Chinese gemstones were of a more practical size to be displayed in public life, although they too were certainly very large. Most of them ranged between 10 and 20 carats, as I recall, which is about as big a stone as a person is likely to be able to wear without listing to port. In addition there were pendants, lavalieres, clips, and bracelets that were an inch and even two inches wide, each set with the finest of diamonds and precious colored stones, and each a tribute to the craftsman who designed it.

A specially privileged handful from the Provident, who attended the World's Fair, not only saw the public display of the House of Jewels but were invited to examine it more closely in a private showing. The reason for the extraordinary courtesy was that the DeBeers representatives in this country had for some time been attending the Provident's auction sales, both to keep an eye on prices and to bolster them if our auction results were ever to flag too much and imperil the stability of the general market. The fact is that diamonds were particularly strong at our sales just then, because of the dealers' fear that imports from Amsterdam and Antwerp might dry up, so the DeBeers group never did feel it necessary to spring into action.

Anyhow, a few of us, whom the DeBeers people knew on a personal basis, were afforded this unusual opportunity to see and handle the superb Chinese collection among the other wonderful jewelry in the display. It would be an obtuse trained appraiser indeed who, once he had seen the collection that closely, would ever forget what it contained.

Two years later, when several magnificent pieces of jewelry were discreetly offered to us for a loan, it was no mystery to guess where they came from. Even without the additional tiny clue that the gentleman seeking the loan was Chinese, the articles were completely recognizable as being among those we had seen in 1939. The gentleman said that he had heard that the Society was basically in business to help the needy with small loans, and was this true? Of course, the answer was a resounding "yes." The Provident will never

make a very large loan if, in doing so, it depletes its funds
so that the small, needy borrower has to be turned away.
The gentleman understood this, but would the Society consider making really quite a large loan, despite this guiding
principle, if its funds were ample? Once again the answer
was "yes." Although it has often set a maximum loan figure
for itself, there have been times when the Society has had
sufficient funds to accommodate the large borrower without
penalizing the small one. This was one of those times, for the
cash drawer was overflowing.

So, for a short period of time, the entire Chinese collection that had been the showpiece of the World's Fair House
of Jewels reposed in the Society's vault, while the Chinese
gentleman went off with his loan ticket and the $135,000 that
he had asked for and received. I would presume that the
retail worth of that collection at that time must have been
at least $1 million, and today it would more probably be
several millions. The specific sum of $135,000 was all that
the pledger wanted, and it was an eminently safe loan from
the Society's standpoint. What the money was used for, or
where the money came from when the collection was redeemed and reclaimed a year later, are not the sort of questions that the Society asks.

But word of some sort inevitably gets around on so unusual a loan as this, and it was only days after the redemption
of the Chinese jewelry that an Egyptian showed up at the
Executive Office. He said he had heard of the Chinese transaction, and was the Society prepared to make some comparable sort of large loan to him? Certainly it was, provided
he had sufficient collateral and satisfactory credentials of
ownership. He produced both from an inner pocket of his

suit. The collateral was a diamond tiara and a matching diamond necklace of the rarest quality, and quite adequate for the $70,000 loan he was seeking. The credentials of ownership were signed by King Farouk's queen, duly dated and attested, and named the Egyptian gentleman as her agent in this matter. One wonders what the purpose of this loan must have been. Was it possible that Farouk had cut down on her household allowance? In any event, as in almost all cases where really astonishing jewels have been in the Provident's custody, the tiara and necklace were soon redeemed, never to go on the auction block.

Shortly after Pearl Harbor I entered the Army and left The Provident Loan Society forever. A few months later the Society received a medium-size package from a military base in Montana. It was accompanied by nothing except a letter asking for "the maximum loan that could be extended on the enclosed."

The wrappings were extraordinarily stout, and the entire package had been put together and wrapped with the utmost care. Inside was an elaborate fitted box, containing some sort of complicated instrument that appeared to involve optics and perhaps chemistry.

No one in the mail room, or in the Fourth Avenue local office, housed on the ground floor of the Executive Office Building, could even begin to guess what it might be. So up it was sent to Munroe Bates on the fourth floor. After all, what use is the head of the Appraisal Department if he can't appraise everything?

Munroe's college degree was in mechanical engineering,

but even he couldn't conceive what this might be. It was wildly harder to imagine how its many parts should be fitted together than in any "build-your-own" apparatus ever foisted on a gullible mail-order purchaser. And it was not even accompanied by an incomprehensible set of directions. However, there was a plate affixed to the bottom of the fitted box that indicated the instrument had been manufactured by a firm in Long Island City, which was no more than half an hour away. Munroe sent off one of the Society's very best men, Jim Werhle, to find out what he could about the article, and to determine whether it was something on which a loan could be made. This was in midmorning.

In the late afternoon Werhle had not been heard from, and Bates became concerned. The Long Island City firm was not listed in the telephone directory, and the telephone company had not been able to supply information about any unlisted number. Just then Bates's own phone rang, and Werhle was on the other end of the wire. He was in control of his voice, but it hovered between nervousness and fury.

"I've been detained here for five hours by Naval Intelligence, ever since this company alerted them to the fact I was here with this damned thing. Now they're allowing me one telephone call, as if I were a criminal. *Do* something!"

Despite a naturally sympathetic nature, Munroe couldn't help laughing. "You won't be detained much longer," he said. "I'm sure our story is adequate, and when they're told the entire affair you'll be released."

"Damn it, I have told them the whole story. I don't think they believe me. When am I going to get something to eat? Will I get to go home tonight? Please call my wife and tell her what's going on and that I can't help it!"

Munroe promised to do everything right away. He first called Naval Intelligence in downtown New York. An hour or so later, Jim was let go and hopefully got home in time for a late dinner. Meanwhile, Bates stayed on at the office by request of the Navy, and then the F.B.I. stepped into the picture. Two agents arrived after the office was closed, and were let in by Munroe.

They asked him to have the article returned to the sender, and to let them know in what mail it went off so that they could have someone ready to arrest the sender when the package arrived back in Montana. Bates replied that the Society wasn't prepared to act in quite so arbitrary a manner, having its own obligations to potential pledgers. Besides, if this was indeed as hush-hush a matter as the F.B.I. implied, it was unreasonable to send the package out into the blue without knowing whether the original sender would indeed be at the base to receive it. First, Bates thought, the Provident should write him for instructions, saying that no loan was possible on the article.

The F.B.I. agreed to that, and Bates carried through. Back came a letter saying that the package should be returned to Montana. When it was, an F.B.I. man was standing in the post office to corral the recipient the moment he claimed it.

Maybe it was a new disinfectant for the barracks. Maybe it had something to do with the atomic bomb. In any case, Bates got a brief note some time later from the man who had sent us the device. It merely said, "Somebody talks too much."

Meanwhile, back at the auction rooms at Silo's, the effects of the outbreak of the war in Europe were staggering. Most critical was the pall of gloom and fear that seeped over the dealers, the majority of whom had friends and relatives in those exact areas the Nazi armor had overcome so rapidly. No news was bad news, for it implied that loved people might well be in concentration camps, or wounded, starving, or dead. Apart from that, like all Americans at that time, everyone at Silo's—from the dealers, through the Provident and the auction gallery staff, to the private buyers—sensed the ominous clouds gathering. It would only be a matter of time before we ourselves would be at war.

On sales days, however, the big picture was sometimes over-shadowed by the small, while the Society's sales went on as usual. Fearful of the effect of the European war upon imports of diamonds, and the curtailment of lapidary activity in the diamond-cutting centers on the Continent, the dealers went berserk endeavoring to buy up as much as they could while the supply lasted. Diamond prices per carat escalated incredibly during those later months of 1939 and throughout 1940. It was particularly true on melee, which is the term for very small diamonds used in diamond wedding rings, watch bracelets, and to flank larger stones in rings. The cutting of melee was not lucrative enough to interest American lapidaries, and practically all of it was imported from Amsterdam. Now it seemed that avenue of purchase was about to be closed, perhaps forever, and the dealers fought with each other to buy up whatever appeared in the Society's sale, almost regardless of whether the quality was good or not.

To a lesser extent, but still to a very marked one, the prices of larger diamonds shot up as well. For the first time in its history, the Society suffered practically no losses at all on diamond loans sold at auction, and the surplus amounts paid out to the borrowers after each sale were immensely big by any previous standard of comparison. Merely from an economic point of view, these were good times for some, such as the recipients of surpluses. For others they were precarious or downright bad times. The dealers, in particular, were not happy about having to pay outlandish wholesale prices when the upward move in retail prices was by no means so immediate or so steep. Eventually that did catch up, but wholesale diamond merchants, as a general rule, are content with small profits and survive on a quick turnover. Back in 1940 they were often stuck too long with inventory they had purchased at our sales. Unable to sell to the next customer along the line in a short space of time, they were beset by the problem of keeping liquid cash reserves.

The result was hitherto unprecedented. After this situation had been going on for some months, several of the important dealers at our auctions no sooner paid their bills at Silo's than they would bundle up their new acquisitions and take them to the nearest Provident Loan Society branch office. There they would get back in hand at least a substantial part of the money they had just paid out. Then, knowing what they had sitting in the Society's vaults, they would redeem specific articles only as the demand for them arose. Additionally, figuring that the climb in diamond prices was not likely to stop for a long time to come, they had a safeguard in mind should they fail to find buyers for their stored goods. After all, if they didn't redeem their loans, the Provident would offer what they had purchased at another sale a year later. Then it would probably fetch even more, and the dealer would reap a surplus that could well not only compensate for the interest the Provident would collect, and the loss of the use of his money for a year, but also throw out a reasonable profit for the dealer.

After Pearl Harbor, with the United States now an active participant in World War II, there was a new consideration to deal with at the Silo sales, and it fell to me to try to handle it, although not for very long since soon afterward I was in the Army. Beginning with the December 1941 sale, there was always a very real possibility that an air-raid warning would sound, in which case everyone was to make his or her way instantly to the many designated shelters that had been established all over New York City. Apart from the gruesome personal fear of a possible bomb attack, we of the Provident had an additional practical problem on our hands if the sirens sounded at all, whether there was an actual attack or whether it was nothing but a practice alert: How could we best safeguard hundreds of valuable articles, worth hundreds of thousands of dollars, all spread out within a crowded room that might be a scene of haste and turmoil at best, and perhaps real panic at worst?

It was my practice to write a long report about each month's sale for my bosses, and here is an excerpt from the December 1941 one: "We have been instructed by the Police that, in case of an air-raid warning, everyone should go immediately to the shelter in the building. As a result, I have formulated the following rules for the Silo personnel to carry out in such an event.

"At the public exhibitions, when articles are spread throughout the counters for the most effective display, the practice is for only one article to be permitted for a customer's inspection at a time. If a person leaves the showcase to ask me a question, he does not bring the article with him.

He returns it to the Silo attendant to be restored to the show-case. Therefore, all that is necessary on those days is for the Silo attendant to get back the article(s) he happens to have out at that moment, which is usually no more than half a dozen or so, and put it (them) back in the tray where they belong. He need not stop to make a count, for these trays are always arranged in neat rows and columns, and a missing item would immediately be apparent. Then each attendant is to collect the trays for which he's responsible, nest one upon the other, and deposit them in the Silo vault. This is a comparatively simple process, and it should not take more than three minutes to execute, including the closing and locking of the vault.

"After the public exhibitions are over, I am having the Silo people cut down on the number of trays by tightening up the way articles are put down in them. Attractive display is desirable at the public exhibitions, and we are likely to place only twenty rings, let us say, in a tray in five rows and four columns. Once the public exhibition days have passed, there is no longer any need for so much empty space in the trays. On dealer days, entire trays are taken by each dealer to his respective table, and the more items in each tray the bet-ter, from his standpoint. Therefore almost two trays can be consolidated into one at that time, by laying out rings in seven rows and five columns.

"Using this method generally, fifteen trays were cut down to nine. Although the trays look less attractive, a pattern still exists which will enable an attendant to check a tray's com-pleteness with a glance, and collect it and the others under his custody in a hurry.

"On each day of the actual sale, we will no longer remove

everything scheduled to be sold from the vault, as has been our practice, but only bring out one tray at a time as the sale progresses. Once an item has actually been auctioned off, the Society's responsibility for its safeguarding is really at an end, but Silo's is carrying out the general idea by replacing the sold items into trays laid out into tighter patterns, with each to go back into the vault immediately upon its being filled up.

"All of this places a slight additional burden on the staff, but the Silo organization is understandably eager to cooperate on ideas of this sort. Additionally, while the physical responsibility of sale items reposes in Silo's hands, and their insurance would make us whole on our loans, our own moral and practical obligations to pledgers makes us at least equally anxious to protect the jewelry, should unusual circumstances like an air-raid alert arise."

After all that, I can only report what didn't happen. New York was never bombed during the war. Nor was any air-raid practice alert ever pulled off while the exhibitions or the sales were taking place.

But our world was coming apart at the seams in England, on the Continent, in Africa, Malaysia, the Phillipines, and Honolulu. And the life that had fascinated me for a decade no longer seemed to be so very important.

✳

CHAPTER 10

Pop Goes the Weasel!

Each new generation inherits a world it never made. A combination of the law of averages and the balance between good and bad luck seems to make things work out fairly evenly. Fate is not likely to favor or frown on one set of lifetimes much more than another. I came to maturity at the bottom of the great Depression of the 1930's, followed by a World War in which I was actively engaged. It wasn't until I was in my mid-thirties that I was completely able to reach out for what I might reasonably have anticipated my good life could be.

My children have never known want or deprivation, but they were born into an age where the atomic-war sword of Damocles has constantly hung over their heads and the unspeakable Vietnam War took place. Now we are plunged into a time of anxiety for the desperate ecological needs of much of the planet, and no young person with a brain and a conscience can be criticized for feeling that he or she may not belong to the luckiest of generations.

Yet anyone with historical perspective knows that man's

ingenuity and fortitude invariably manage to overcome each threat to civilization in the end, and I think the same will happen for my children. Our generation's ideals of proper human conduct for those in positions of responsibility received a considerable jolt in 1938 when we saw the rich aristocrocratic President of the Stock Exchange convicted of embezzling funds and sent off to jail for three years. How much more shattering it must be for present-day young people to come to maturity just as another President is shown to have betrayed his trust much more grievously. Yet the Stock Exchange has survived, and Richard Whitney was an all but forgotten name for almost forty years, until his obituary appeared late in 1974. The United States of America will survive too, and while Richard Nixon's name will not be forgotten, it won't be remembered very well forty years from now. If that opinion stamps me as a Pollyanna, so be it. I am an unabashed optimist as far as the long-range picture is concerned, even if immediate circumstances are extremely dire.

We deal in daily life with the short range, however, and now a painful recession is upon us that bids fair to rival the Depression of which I write. Pawnbroking in general, and The Provident Loan Society in particular, have not been major economic forces over the years since I laid down my jeweler's loupe. Credit organizations, banks, and finance companies, most of which don't require collateral, lessened the need for the pledge loan, as long as the nation was enjoying good times. But the hard-pressed self-employed, the unemployed, the retired older person with a small fixed income that allows little or nothing for emergencies, widows and divorcées with children, the hourly and the seasonal worker,

and those who earn little above the poverty wage are classified as poor risks by banks and by other credit and lending
agencies. Major banks don't make loans of less than $500
because of the high administrative cost. The finance companies' small loans have built-in finance charges and life insurance premiums paid by the borrower, which results on the
average in an interest rate of just about 32 percent for a loan
of $100.

The Provident's present interest rate is 1½ percent per
month for the exact number of days on a loan of less than
$100, which is 18 percent per annum. On loans of more than
$100, the Society now charges 1½ percent per month for the
first six months and 1 percent thereafter, or 15 percent per
annum. The interest rate was considerably lower in my day,
but costs, losses, and additional protection safeguards since
the threat of robbery has become so much more acute have
necessitated some rise in interest rates. They still remain the
lowest in the country for this commercial finance type of loan.

So the Society's services have continued to be a lifesaver for
the truly needy who cannot qualify for credit from other
sources. This was, and is after all, its primary mission. There
are but eight offices now where once there were twenty-two,
and the loan balance is only about one-quarter of what it was
in the 1930's. But in the first few years of the 1970's, well
over 40,000 loans a year were still being made to those who
sought them. And as hard times grow constantly harder, there
have been very tangible signs that the Provident is going to
be needed more and more.

This opinion may not be applicable for the future of commercial pawnbrokers, because circumstances have created a
very paradoxical situation for them. By state law, their in-

terest rates can be 30 percent per year on loans of $100 or less, and 18 percent on loans over $100, and that's what they charge. Far from being able to charge less interest, commercial pawnbrokers have found that they cannot make out well, or even make out at all these days, and there have been intense but to date futile efforts by their association to have legal pawnbroking interest rates increased in order for them to survive. As one pawnbroker put it in late 1974, "We are paying about 14 percent to get our money on which to operate. That gives us a 4 percent margin on loans over $100. We just can't do it on 4 percent." A spectacular example of what the commercial pawnbroker has been up against came in October 1973 when Kaskel's, on West 57th Street just off Fifth Avenue, had to go out of the pawnbroking business. Kaskel's, long known as the millionaire's pawnshop that specialized in large loans, did not own its building but rented it. When the rent jumped very substantially and Kaskel's was already faced with the problems outlined above, it was the straw that broke the camel's back. Kaskel's had to throw in the towel.

Certainly all the smaller pawnbrokers today, and even a comparatively large and long established one such as R. Simpson & Co. on midtown Fifth Avenue, feel that legal interest rates are such that they have to conduct their affairs in quite the opposite manner than Kaskel's did. They do not want to make a $500 loan on which they can only charge 18 percent. They would much prefer to make five $100 loans instead, despite the additional paperwork and storage problems, because they can collect 30 percent on those.

The Provident Loan Society manages to survive without having to resort to comparable operations, since the difference between its interest rate on small and large loans isn't nearly as great, and because it does not have to borrow money to keep going. In today's economic climate of easy credit, the Society and the pawnbroker both know that they cannot compete in large areas of the business of extending loans. The pledge loan requires taking over physical possession of property, storing it and caring for it, as well as the expertise required in judging its value. The loan officer of a personal finance company, or a commercial bank, can sit in one small room with a desk and complete an entire transaction with the signing of some papers and the issuance of a check. He will levy liens or notes on personal property, but he does not ever even see it, let alone have to accept it and take it over for safekeeping. His judgment about the solidity of a credit risk is all that he needs.

If a person has credit standing, much can be said for using such facilities. The great virtue of the pledge loan, as practiced by pawnshops and The Provident Loan Society, is that it's open to everybody, including those who need it most, without investigation, co-signers, embarrassment, and possible refusal. Certainly, in the case of the Provident, it is felt that it still can render service to so substantial a segment of the city's society, in a manner that no other organization can match, that it will be a long time before it need not exist any longer. But as a sober correlation, there were more than 150 commercial pawnshops in New York City forty years ago. By the mid-1950's the number was down to 130, and today there are only about 35. It seems reasonably certain that the pledge loan will never be as extensive as it once was, but it appears equally sure that it still can and will perform a vital function not matched by other forms of lending.

My own career with the Society came to an end in the early 1940's, which means that I missed a lot of the fun that was introduced later, when certain types of collateral became acceptable for the first time.

The thought of expanding in this direction had crossed our minds even back during the Depression, but after Munroe Bates had done some reconnaissance investigation into some of the practices of commercial pawnbrokers, the idea was dropped. He visited a major pawnshop in the Bronx, for example, to inquire about how it handled loans on clothing. He was told that when a person offered his suit or overcoat, a loan of $10 or $15 was agreed upon, the ticket was written, and then the clothing was tossed in a heap upon a counter, or even the floor. The man was asked if he wanted to have "special treatment," which ranged from simply having the article hung up to having it brushed thoroughly before being put on a hanger. If he said that he did, he was charged an extra 25 cents or even more. The net effect was quite profitable for the pawnshop, for those were invariably short-term loans that were repeated, week after week, each time with a new charge. Usually they were a man's best clothes, which he did not dare leave in a room he shared with someone else whom he might not even know. In Harlem at that time there were twenty-four-hour "hot beds," where three men took successive eight-hour shifts with no change in linen. It was very hazardous to leave anything around that could be stolen, and that accounted for many of the pawnbroker's clothing loans.

Munroe Bates was understandably unimpressed, and the notion of accepting clothing as collateral was dropped.

However, in 1948 the Provident did decide that making

loans on furs might be something else again. With its inevitable attention to doing things the proper way, three branch offices were selected to receive furs, one each in Manhattan, Brooklyn, and the Bronx. Refrigerated vaults were established there for proper storage. One appraiser from each of the three offices was sent for a year's intermittent training course in fur knowledge and values to the now defunct but then prestigious Gunther-Jaeckel Furs. At the end of that time the offices were ready for such business.

Over the next twenty years the Provident did indeed extend loans, from the cheapest lapin through Persian lamb and Hudson seal, all the way to magnificent mink and sable coats. To the best of my informant's memory, they never took in a chinchilla, but you can't have everything. The fact is that, in the end, the Society came to think that it would be better off not to accept furs as collateral at all, for it was not the happiest of experiences all the way down the line.

To begin with, at the time of a loan the appraiser had to get the customer's permission to use a pair of scissors and open up the lining of the coat. This was a request that often was not greeted with warm enthusiasm, but it was necessary in order to be able to feel a fur's quality, whether it had dried out, and vital matters of that sort. But let's say a loan was finally effected, ranging from perhaps $10 through a great many in the hundreds of dollars, to as much as $5,000 on one occasion. A fur coat did indeed require the Provident's conscientious and costly form of special handling and special storage. If the item was redeemed later, well and good.

But if a year went by and the article was let go to auction sale, catastrophe was no infrequent visitor. Styles change very quickly in the fur trade, and furs—unlike diamonds—are not forever. The $500 loan in 1951, on a coat easily worth $650 to $750 at that time, could in 1952 well be something no woman would be seen dead in. The losses incurred in furs at the auctions were proportionately the most severe that the Provident ever suffered, possibly excepting big pearl loans.

In the late 1960's, when the Bronx and Brooklyn offices were closed, the Manhattan office at Times Square was the only one left that still had facilities for furs, and it was decided that the right moment had come to call quits to a bad thing.

Loans on stamps and coins, which also became acceptable collateral at The Provident Loan Society only over the past thirty years or so, have proven to be much sounder. Once again, the sciences of philately and numismatics require the trained knowledge of an expert, and all such loans of any importance are referred to the Executive Office. There the prospective borrower will be escorted to see George Smith, who has devoted his career to becoming just such an expert. Starting with the Society as a cashier at the age of eighteen, George has been there forty-five years and claims to have loved every minute of it. He must have had a certain amount of company as well, for the *average* working life of the Provident's male employees over its history is thirty-five years! A person like myself, who dropped in and stayed for ten years, is remembered as a fairly casual visitor.

George Smith has offered this explanation for why people bring stamps to the Provident: "We have granted loans to philatelists for sums ranging from five dollars to ten thousand dollars. We take as pledges all United States mint stamps. There have been a few isolated occasions where we have taken some British Colonies, although this is the exception rather than the rule. We prefer to handle only United States mint.

"We claim the lowest known interest rates, and people are sometimes a little squeamish about getting money from a loan corporation or a bank because of the personal investigation involved. Not that the individual has anything to hide, but he just doesn't like the idea of having friends or relatives contacted for credit information or having to be embarrassed by obtaining co-signers. Here we make no investigation in matters of this sort. If the prospective pledger can show he owns the mint stamps free from encumbrances, we can make the loan.

"The collection, after being sealed, is not reopened until its release back to the pledger. It is locked away in vaults used only for this purpose. In these vaults the individual's stamps are kept in better condition than it is possible for any private person to keep them. We constantly check humidity and temperature to prevent deterioration and discoloration."

The Society started to take in stamps five years after I left, so I have no personal anecdotes to tell about them. What is more, the sort of dramatic story, such as can now be told about a famous diamond, should not be revealed in a comparable case involving a rare stamp. Loans on such stamps are likely to be repeated, sometimes again and again, and information about the location of especially valuable stamps is guarded closely among philatelists. However, there is one charming reminiscence that George has felt free to relate.

One time, a soft-spoken and neatly dressed woman, her eyes red from weeping, presented a box at the Provident's office. It contained her stamp collection, and she was seeking a $350 loan on it.

Smith evaluated the contents of the box and agreed to the amount. Hearing his favorable decision, she burst into tears. George asked her if he could do anything for her.

"No," she said, "it's just that I'm going to have an operation tomorrow. That's why I need the money now."

"Oh, you'll be all right," Smith said in an effort to console her. "Those surgeons do wonders nowadays."

She looked up. "I'm afraid not," she said. "It's—cancer."

The woman never returned to renew or redeem her loan, and a little over a year later Smith saw the stamps sold at a Provident auction.

"I really didn't know her at all," he recalled, "but somehow I felt really sad. She loved those stamps. I knew that if she had lived, she'd have come in to redeem them. I hated to see the story end that way.

"But, in fact, it didn't. Several years later she walked in here big as life. She had been ill and unable to redeem her loan, but now she was completely cured and felt fine again. She only came to the office to tell me, and because she thought I'd like to know that she was going to start collecting stamps again."

The Provident Loan Society made an interesting discovery in the early 1950's. It had not come to its notice before that the Borough of Queens, across the river there on Long Island, was a part of the city of Greater New York. Its population had skyrocketed in the post-war years. The staggering idea emerged that it might well be possible that people in Queens needed loans just as much as people in Manhattan, Brooklyn and the Bronx.

A simple one-room office was rented in Jamaica, originally merely to answer inquiries, refer prospective pledgers to existing offices in the other boroughs, and ascertain how much interest there might be in the permanent establishment of a Jamaica office. After a couple of years of such record keeping, it seemed clear that demand for a local Long Island branch office did indeed exist. The Society then proceeded to institute one of the more imaginative and untypical actions of its long history.

Purchasing a large General Motors bus, they had all the interior equipment ripped out. A safe was then installed behind a long counter, over which was mounted a barricade separating the public-space part of the bus from the safe. An appraiser, who had to double in brass as cashier and vault-man as well, worked in the space alongside the safe. A second employee was the driver of the bus, and his only other function was its maintenance.

Christened "The Loanmobile," it did not proceed along the expressways of Long Island, ringing a little bell and hawking its services like a Good Humor wagon. Instead, early each morning it settled in at available parking sites in key Long Island locations. On Mondays the Loanmobile would be at its Forest Hills location; on Tuesdays in Woodside; on Wednesdays, Flushing; on Thursdays, Ozone Park; and on Fridays, Bayside.

The collateral taken in by the Loanmobile was temporarily placed in its safe. Later it was taken to the Jamaica office for more permanent storage while in the Society's custody. The tickets that were written out in the Loanmobile, at the time loans were made, were issued for the Jamaica office, and redemptions had to be made there. From June 1952 to September 1954 the Loanmobile pursued its peripatetic course around Queens with gratifying results, justifying the opening of a true Jamaica office, at which time the Loanmobile was retired to pasture.

The Jamaica office did nicely enough, once it was established, and it would just have taken its sober place in history beside all the other branch offices had it not been the target of the huge robbery described in the Prologue of this book. That event not only traumatized the serenity of the Trustees and the administrative officers, but led them to take steps that had never been considered necessary previously. It is true that petty larceny attempts had been essayed before on the Society's premises. The nature of the business, embracing as it does both cash and small valuables, inevitably brings to the surface the temptation to rip off something. For example, individuals have been caught poking canes tipped with chewing gum through the wickets in branch offices, trying to latch onto a ring on the counter. Also, during the exhibition days at the auction sales, there would occasionally be cases where a minor portion of an article was nipped off by someone pretending to inspect the item. The absence of a dangling part of a pendant, or an end of a gold chain, would not be too likely to be noticed as the bulk of an article was restored to the tray. Anyhow, this sort of infrequent thing was usually spotted and nipped in the bud. On the even more infrequent number of cases where it wasn't, the single loss incurred was a modest one, and the Society was insured at least for the amount of the loan. Further satisfaction to the pledger was accomplished by replacement, and any actual cash loss could justifiably be termed a normal business risk. Every organization has to face this type of loss in one way or the other, and allows for it in budgeting a fiscal year.

But the balloon really went up with the robbery of the Jamaica office in 1969, involving over 3,000 articles worth $4 to $6 million. A different set of rules for playing the game had to be drawn up as quickly as possible. It had become evident that the new age of violence was no respecter of persons, or of institutions. The proof that fresh safeguards were absolutely necessary, and not merely the panicky reaction to one unprecedented and perhaps never-to-be-repeated calamity, came when the East 60th Street Office suffered another robbery, albeit much smaller, within months after the Jamaica office theft.

So today a whole set of precautions simply must exist. The Society's vaults are more solid and burglar-proof than they ever were, and are still as safe a place as anyone could find and rely upon for the safekeeping of valuables. But the Jamaica and East 60th Street experiences brought home the hitherto unthinkable fact that, looking at the wrong end of a weapon, anyone is likely to be persuaded to open a vault or empty a cash drawer. The Provident does carry insurance, but only for the amount it loans on articles. Therefore collecting any such insurance would reimburse the Provident but achieve nothing toward making the pledger whole for the loss of property that almost invariably had a much greater value than the loan he had obtained. Yet for the Society to insure collateral for sums several times the size of the respective loan amounts is completely impracticable. The premiums would be of a magnitude that would require a fantastic increase in the interest rates the Provident charges pledgers.

A loan ticket today bears a notation that never used to exist before what a mystery author would title "The Affair of the Jamaica Office." It reads: "Collateral not insured. Not responsible for loss or damage by fire, water, riot, burglary, robbery, theft or any loss or damage caused by any other casualty." If this somber warning were to discourage you from turning to the Provident in your next financial hour of need, think again. It is no more cautious than the legal boiler-plate clauses that exist in just about every contract one signs. It's there to protect the Provident in case of another major, sweeping catastrophe, like the Jamaica one, which it may be powerless to prevent. If the Society itself were to be responsible for the loss or damage to your piece of jewelry, my guess is it would accept the responsibility of replacing the loss or rectifying the damage. That was its stance in my years there, and it seems to me that its moral outlook is as strong as it ever was.

The new physical safeguards that have been installed in the offices cost money and have been a major factor in the nesessity to raise interest rates. The other significant factors have been increased overhead costs and unusual losses at the auction sales.

As far as overhead is concerned, it has not been a matter of the Society plunging into new and expensive operations. No market research consultants. And, believe it or not, just about everything is still carried out manually. True, there are a couple of electronic calculators around the place, and photocopying machines. But writing tickets, computing interest, recording the history of a loan not only on the ticket but also on the accompanying police inventory tags are all done by hand. *Practically no error is ever made!* (There may be a lesson in this.) The very fact that people work so conscientiously and well, for so many years at the Provident, means that seniority is recognized more than in most businesses when it comes to salary adjustment time. In the inflationary spiral of recent years, up goes the overhead.

Two examples will illustrate the type of unusual auction sale loss that the Society is likely to suffer. A manufacturer of certain office equipment found himself desperately in need of cash. He came to the Provident Loan office and showed a sample, desk-size calculating machine, which listed in his catalogue at a retail price over $100. He claimed that all he was seeking was an accommodation loan for a short period of time, and that he would redeem the machines immediately after he had employed the cash profitably. There seemed no good reason not to lend the $35 he asked on such a machine, and that figure was agreed upon. Unfortunately, the appraiser who made the determination never realized how many of these calculators the man had, and how quickly he would pour them into the various local branches once the authorized sum had been set and distributed to the offices. The fact is that he pledged something like 100 of them, moving from office to office on different days, and returning after an interval to present still other machines to an appraiser who hadn't seen him last time. When he never returned to redeem any of them, they all showed up at the auction rooms, scheduled to be sold at very nearly the same time. If there had only been three or four of them, undoubtedly the person then in charge of the sales would have recommended spreading them out, one to be sold at a time over the ensuing months. But 100 calculating machines could not be swept under the rug, nor could any such great number be postponed to later sales. That would take years, and certainly not be worth it. The Society swallowed hard and offered a substantial number of them at the first sale.

When an auction audience sees a quantity of items about to be put on the block, each exactly like the others, instinct says not to bid on the first few, to wait around to see what price level is going to be established. That means that bidding is anything from slight to nonexistent on the first lot offered. When the lot has to be knocked down for a very disappointing price, that sort of price is established for the items to follow. If that isn't a vicious circle, it's certainly a vicious boomerang. But enough of this sober story: The calculating machines were sold for about $5 each.

A comparable auction sale loss on bulk goods came when a substantial number of Canadian proof sets of coins were struck off and became popular with numismatists in this country. The face value of the six coins in the set was $1.91, but the Provident understood the coin market well (where they might have been naive about calculating machines) and knew that any collector would be glad to pay $4 for such a set. Accordingly, the sum of $3 per set was authorized as a loan, and many coin dealers took advantage of the offer to obtain more working capital, knowing their coins were stored rather better than they could do it themselves. So what happened soon after a great many of these sets had been pledged and were neatly stacked away in the Provident's vaults? The Canadian Government, seeing that they had a good thing going with their friendly neighbors to the South, reminted and ground out a new mountain of these proof sets. The bottom dropped out of the premium aspect of their value, and they became worth just about $1.91 again.

What's the story on The Provident Loan Society's auction sales today? Readers who perhaps have been intrigued by the incredible bargains obtainable in days of yore may wonder if comparable opportunities exist now. Well . . . yes and no.

Silo's auction rooms have gone the way of the nickel cup of coffee, but regular Provident Loan Society auctions still take place. They only occur three or four times a year, instead of monthly, and even so they are much smaller than they once were. But they still engender a lot of interest and fascination. They are conducted on the premises of the Plaza Art Auction Galleries, way east on 79th Street, and a request to The Provident Loan Society will put you on the mailing list to be notified about upcoming auctions.

Prices realized there are so much higher than when I knew them that I recoil in amazement, but that is the reaction of a dinosaur to the 20th century. All I can report is that just as many dealers—wholesale dealers from West 47th Street—patronize those sales as did in my day. They are not naive, and if they feel that the prices at Provident Loan sales make participation in those sales a good thing, it's still every bit as good a thing for the private buyer as it once was, in comparative terms. I have attended a couple of exhibitions and sales in recent times, and even if you are not a serious bidder, it's still good fun. I recommend at least going and taking a look. It's as good as browsing in Madison Avenue galleries, and if you decide to buy something, and if inflation continues, you undoubtedly will be able to acquire jewelry at much less than you would have to pay in a retail establishment.

All the eleemosynary aspects of the Provident's good works continue. No profits go into anyone's pockets. As of the close of business in 1974, $3.5 million had been distributed to the charities of New York over the years. Well over $5 million had been paid to pledgers in auction sale surpluses realized over and above the sums they had borrowed. And $1.7 million had been turned over to the State of New York in surpluses unclaimed by pledgers, to be held in trust forever while awaiting claimants.

There has been no time in recorded history when the lending of money in return for a pledged security has not been the major last resource for the needy. The Emperor Augustus Caesar founded such a business as far back as 31 B.C., and he may not have been the first pawnbroker by any means. Through centuries, whenever people have been in financial distress, the pledge loan has been a lifesaver. Americans today do not realize it, but more than a century ago this point was immortalized in an old English song, the original meaning of which has been lost in the translation into verses for children.

The American child learns words to "Pop Goes the Weasel!" that indicate that the weasel is a little animal being chased around a cobbler's bench by a fun-loving monkey. "Pop!" conveys the idea that the weasel either pops up or is popped off by the monkey. It depends upon how jolly, or sadistic, the child's imagination is.

Neither interpretation has anything to do with the thought behind every verse of the original English song, which is attributed to W. R. Mondale. At that time, about 1853—and still—"pop" was a term meaning to pawn, the equivalent of "to hock." And "Weasel" was the slang term for a flatiron used to press clothing. The first two lines of each verse told of the spending habits everyone had, sometimes necessary ones and sometimes pleasurable ones. The third line was always "That's the way the money goes—" and the last line, of course, was the familiar "Pop Goes the Weasel!" *Viz:* When one's money was gone, it was off to the pawnshop with one's flatiron.

Here are a few verses from that version:

> A penny for a spool of thread
> A penny for a needle,
> That's the way the money goes—
> Pop goes the weasel!

> Potatoes for an Irishman's taste
> The doctor for the measles,
> That's the way the money goes—
> Pop goes the weasel!

> Up and down the City Road,
> In and out the Eagle,*
> That's the way the money goes—
> Pop goes the weasel!

There are not so many places where the weasel can be popped anymore, although both the pawnshops and The Provident Loan Society may grow again as, and if, our recession turns into a real depression. Good financial times breed easy credit. But bad times, when the needy can turn nowhere else, evoke the "God Bless Pawnbrokers" feeling.

For this book, and also out of a combination of curiosity and nostalgia, I rented a drive-your-own car and made a sweep of the city, following the routes as best I remembered them when I was driven by the chauffeur in the Society's

* The Eagle was a pub or music hall on the City Road.

limousine. I decided to skip the Jamaica office, which I had never had any contact with, but I slowly steered through the traffic of the three boroughs of the city where the twenty-two offices that I had known once had been located.

I started in Brooklyn. Only one of the four offices that existed in the 1930's is still there, looking much as it always did on Church Avenue in the residential area of Flatbush. Both the old Williamsburg office at Graham Avenue and Debevoise Street, and the Brownsville one on Pitkin Avenue have become furniture stores, which may mean something significant about modern Brooklyn but, if so, I can't fathom it. The once most important of the Brooklyn offices, dubbed "Brooklyn" for that very reason and located on Livingston Street near the heart of Borough Hall, has been demolished, and on its site a new courthouse now stands.

Working my way across the river to Manhattan, I drove up through the canyons of the Wall Street area to where the Fulton Street Office, west of Broadway and opposite St. Paul's Chapel, had been. It was pleasant to spot it still standing there, and gratifying to me, a book publisher these many years, to see that its new incarnation was as a bookstore. However the old City Hall Office, one of the few established on the ground floor of a then new office building, had given way over the years to a succession of quick lunch spots, ranging from a spaghetti house to a Nedick's orange drink stand that looks out over Foley Square—next time I'm on jury duty and hard pressed for time to eat lunch, I'll try it for old time's sake.

It was only a matter of wending my way a few blocks east and north, through and past Chinatown, to be able to view what was, or rather what was not, left of the three Lower

East Side offices that once had served the ghetto community so well. The Eldridge Street Office is gone, and instead there is a school of adult education. The Grand Street Office has given way to a cooperative housing development. And the East Houston Street Office, originally sold to a synagogue, is now a sort of studio, or warehouse, for massive pieces of sculpture. Peeking through the windows I saw huge angular free-form statuary such as would make Henry Moore wonder why he executed such tidy neat little stuff.

Feeling somewhat depressed, I drove uptown and was heartened to see that my old basic stamping ground, the Executive Office at 346 Fourth Avenue (excuse me, Postmaster General, 346 Park Avenue South) was looking exactly the same at the corner of 25th Street. There was even someone outside, polishing the brass knobs of the big front door.

Turning west and moving uptown a bit further, the construction of the new Madison Square Garden and Penn Plaza have wiped out the old 33rd Street Penn Station branch office. In the huge, modernistic complex that now dominates the block, it's hard to zero in on any X that marks the spot where the Society's building stood, but I tend to think it's a new Bowery Savings Bank.

Miraculously spared by the years, the Grand Central Office on 43rd Street, east of Lexington Avenue, appeared to be unchanged and thriving, but the once equally prosperous East 47th Street one, near Madison Avenue, is now "Maggie's Place," the most recent of a series of counter-and-stool eateries housed there in recent years.

The Times Square Office on Seventh Avenue, near 49th Street, seems to be the real Rock of Gibraltar of the survivors. It was always the biggest office, doing the most business, and that seems still to be true. It is probably one of the few edifices in the Times Square environs that a visitor to the district, from forty years ago, would recognize at once as being unchanged, although it has had some cosmetic refacing on its facade. The really startling alteration in the appearance of that block from what used to exist is the hard-core pornography movie house, whose entrance is only a few feet away from the doors of the Provident Loan. When I looked at it recently it was playing a double bill, "Deep Throat" and "The Devil in Miss Jones." Well, that's one of the perils of real estate. You never can know who your neighbors are likely to turn out to be. Linda Lovelace and Georgina Spelvin.

I live on the West Side of New York City, and I knew that the old Provident office that used to exist between Broadway and Columbus Avenue, and which geographically would be my next port of call, had long since been sold and converted into a paint and wallpaper store. If I ever need to pop the family heirlooms, it would now have to be a case of "Go East, Young Man" and seek out the East 72nd Street branch, near Third Avenue, or the East 60th Street one, just off Lexington. Both of them have remained intact, doing business at the old stands in the same old way while new neighbors have sprung up about them. I have seen them often in recent years, when visiting friends on the East Side. So I decided to bypass swinging over there and simply continue to head uptown on the West Side to look into what had happened to the Society's old office, which used to stand on the corner of Eighth Avenue and 127th Street, and then east to the former Mount Morris branch, located at Lexington Avenue and 124th Street.

I'll tell you what's happened to them. The outer shells of both buildings are there, but one has become the Baptist Church of Mount Nebo and the other is now a huge surplus military clothing outlet. Intrigued by the latter, if not the former, I got out and wandered into the store. Almost seduced by a jacket that looked similar to the warmest garment I ever owned, an armored tank jacket I had in World War II, I happened to see the label: "Made in Hong Kong." I passed it up and climbed back into the car.

Finally, I pushed up into the Bronx, where once three offices had flourished. As in Brooklyn, only one remains, the Fordham branch. It is located, much as it was forty years ago, in what is still a middle-to-upper-class residential neighborhood. But, as in the other two boroughs of New York, the offices that once served the very poor have been closed. This would seem to be a direct contradiction of the Provident Loan's founding principle of basically serving the needy —a principle still very much held in mind and honored by the present administration—but it was explained to me why it isn't contradictory. Two related factors have combined to influence the Society to close the offices once situated in what might be termed ghetto districts. For one thing, the respectable poor people who used to cluster together in them, in national or religious groups, now have moved out and are living in low-cost housing units spread all over the city. For the other, those once deprived areas have themselves changed immensely in character. The Lower East Side of Manhattan, for example, was indeed poor but was filled with decent, hardworking Jewish families. It was as safe to stroll along its streets as it was anywhere else in the city forty years ago. These days, however, that sector is what is known as the East

Village, and has one of the highest crime rates in New York. The same is true of certain areas in the Bronx these days, and a place like a Provident Loan Society office, loaded with precious jewelry and cash, might need the National Guard to survive in such locations.

That is why, as I drove back down through the Bronx, I found the other two branch offices formerly set in that borough had also passed into limbo. We had once had a very big and active office in the business heart of the Bronx at 148th Street. The building is still there, looking much as it did, but the sign over its door indicates that it now houses the Bronx office of Consolidated Edison. However, Fate had reserved the biggest jolt to my nostalgic journey for the very end. Driving out along Southern Boulevard to try to locate the old Hunts Point office, I simply could not find it, or anything else recognizable.

Hunts Point never was that easy to find, nor had I visited it in the past as often as I had most of the other branches. It had not been a separate little gem of a one-story edifice, like the overwhelming majority of Provident Loan offices, but had instead been a large ground-floor room, rented by the Society in a fairly large building. Now, as I drove slowly along the boulevard, I might as well have been in a strange, foreign city. Except that I knew better, I would have sworn that I'd never, ever, seen anything around me before. A barren plot of ground, littered with junk, and looking like every other site of that character, could possibly have been where the Hunts Point office had once been, but I had no more real reason for thinking so than I had about a dozen other places. I parked the car and tried asking a few local shopkeepers if they knew anything about the old Provident Loan Society branch that had been somewhere around there. No one had the vaguest idea what I was talking about. It had been a long time ago, after all.

Somewhat moodily, I drove back downtown and returned the rented car just as evening shadows were falling. Walking back to my apartment while night closed in, I thought of things past and wondered if the ghosts of weasels, popped and gone, still haunt the quick lunch counter and the Army-and-Navy store, the Harlem church, and perhaps even the deserted lot. I like to think they do.

About the Author

Born in New York City and educated, in a vague way, at the Lawrenceville School and Princeton University, Peter Schwed then spent almost ten years working for The Provident Loan Society of New York, which gave him the background for this book.

After four years in the army as a field artilleryman in World War II, he joined the book publishing firm of Simon and Schuster in late 1945 and has been there ever since. He became its Publisher for half a dozen years during the last decade, and today is its Chairman of the Editorial Board.

He co-edited a three-volume anthology with Herbert Warren Wind, *Great Stories from the World of Sport,* as well as the massive *Fireside Book of Tennis,* with Allison Danzig. A keen tennis player himself, Mr. Schwed's own book, *Sinister Tennis* (which is about how to play against left-handers as opponents, and with them as doubles partner) was published earlier this year.